Advanced
English Billiards

Advanced English Billiards

Match-winning shots and strategies in the all-round game

Martin Goodwill
&
Roger Morgan

englishBilliards.org

ISBN : 978-0-9564054-4-9

Published by englishBilliards.org
First edition, June 2013
Printed in the United Kingdom

Contents

Lesson Two. **65**
Stun and screw shots

Lesson Three 105
Recovery shots

*A cannon played off a cushion before hitting the first object ball,
in order to make an angle for the shot*

*An in-off played off a cushion before hitting the object ball in
order to make a suitable angle*

Foreword

Tom Cleary, once world and five times Australian amateur champion, toured extensively with Walter Lindrum, serving as punchbag opponent, referee and general factotum. One day, he asked the great man how to play nursery cannons.

"Well, it's touch," said Lindrum.
"I know, Walter, but how do I play them?"
"You've got to practise."

And that was it.

Lindrum either did not want to disclose his secrets or had absorbed the nuanced skills of nursery cannons so subconsciously that he did not care to try to put them into words.

Martin Goodwill, six times English amateur billiards champion, and Roger Morgan, co-founders of *englishBilliards.org*, have completely the opposite attitude: they want to share their considerable knowledge as widely as possible—as they demonstrate in this book.

Advanced English Billiards exhaustively discusses jennies and run-throughs, larger subjects than one might think, screw and stun shots and common recovery shots, both in-offs and cannons. The sections on the effects of the nap and *straightening* the object ball when using check side are more informative than anything that has been published before.

This is a most useful book for those who are already playing billiards at a reasonable level but who now aspire to a deeper understanding of break-building strategies. Even experienced players may learn something new from this book or be reminded of things they have forgotten.

CLIVE EVERTON—EDITOR, *SNOOKER SCENE*

How to use this book

This book has three lessons to teach you shots and strategies to improve your match-winning potential at billiards. To make the quickest progress it is best to follow the lessons in sequence, but if you are using the book to brush up on some aspect of your existing game you should be able to go directly to the required section.

Throughout the book you will find explanations of various concepts, some of which may be new to you. A good understanding of these concepts will be fundamental to your improvement. Often, a concept is followed by a suggested cue drill. Don't be tempted to skip these drills as they will help you to play many of the shots that follow.

Shot diagrams

The thickness of *contact* that should be made on the object ball is indicated (in this case it is about quarter-ball) and the blue circle on the cue ball shows the address that is recommended to make the shot (in this case at the centre of the ball). The length of the blue arrow near the cue ball gives some indication of the recommended strength of the shot, although you can also get an idea of this by noting the final position of the balls. Coloured lines show the paths of the balls and balls outlined in black represent their final positions.

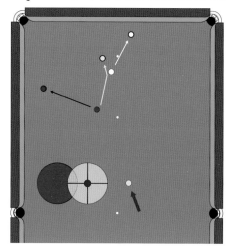

Ball positions

In most cases you should be able to set up the balls simply by looking at the diagrams, but there are a few shots that may require you to set up the balls exactly so that you are confident that you are playing from the correct position. In these cases it would help if you had a tape measure to hand. Unless otherwise stated, measurements have been taken from the face of the cushion (the cloth at the front edge of the cushion) to the centre of the ball, so that you can measure and mark the positions of the balls where necessary. It will help if you have a small piece of white chalk, otherwise rotate your fingertip in the end of a piece of billiard chalk and lightly mark the cloth that way. Occasionally, reference is made to the number of *ball-widths* away from a cushion or a ball; one ball-width away implies that you could just fit one ball between either a cushion or another ball. Throughout this book, when referring to the relative positions of balls, *above* describes a ball which is nearer the top cushion and *below* one nearer the bottom cushion.

When you are playing the shots it is important to practise from both sides of the table. This will help you to see the shots from different aspects and for your eyes to become accustomed to the angles that you will need to judge. It will also help you to avoid establishing a favourite side of the table. Don't forget to adjust the address on the cue ball when playing a shot from the other side of the table. For example, if the address is shown at the bottom left of the cue ball in a shot diagram, you will need to address at bottom right when playing the shot from the other side of the table.

While every effort has been made to ensure the accuracy of the measurements given in this book, you may find that some minor adjustments are required for your particular table because of slight variations in exact table dimensions, cloth types, balls and pocket sizes.

Terminology

You should be familiar with basic terms—*side, follow-through* and *screw*, for example. If in doubt, definitions of billiards terminology can be found at the *englishBilliards.org* website.

Lesson One

Jennies and run-throughs

This lesson is all about shots that make use of sidespin and depend on the effect of the nap.

You will learn the techniques needed to play all types of spinning jenny. These shots make full use of the nap so there's quite a lot of information on how you can use this to your advantage, both for jennies and other shots that are played with sidespin.

Finally, you will learn all about various types of run-through, some of which make use of the nap effect, as well as how to play spinning run-throughs when the object ball is close to the cushion.

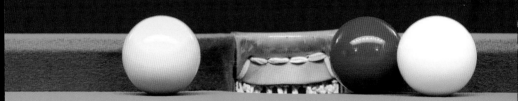

Concept: Sidespin *with* the nap

If you brush your hand along the bed of the table, from the baulk end towards the top end the cloth will feel smooth, but in the opposite direction you will feel the roughness of the cloth. This is because the fibres of the cloth point towards the top cushion—this is the *nap*.

The nap affects so many shots that you need to understand it thoroughly if you are to enjoy a good standard of billiards. As there's quite a lot to absorb, the various effects of the nap are described in separate sections throughout the book.

When a ball is moving towards the top cushion it is said to be travelling *with* the nap and it is travelling *against* the nap when moving towards the baulk cushion. The diagram shows that when travelling *with* the nap, left sidespin (clockwise rotation) causes the cue ball to drift to the left. In the same way, right sidespin would cause it to drift to the right. The cue ball will push off line from the initial impact of the tip and then drift in the direction of the imparted side. You can see this effect more clearly as the ball slows down and approaches the pocket, assuming that it is still spinning sufficiently.

**With the nap, a ball will drift in the same
direction as the applied side**

Of course, the quality of the nap varies considerably from table to table depending on both the type of cloth and how worn it is. The heavier the nap, the more a spinning ball will drift.

A spinning ball will drift about the same amount for paths up to around 45° to the nap. At angles greater than this there is still enough drift to markedly affect the shot and there is still a small amount of drift if the ball's path is nearly across the direction of the nap. Also, a spinning ball will drift more the slower it travels. Fast-moving balls hardly drift at all, even if they are carrying a significant amount of sidespin.

The Short Jenny

A spinning loser into a middle pocket, played when the object ball is near the side cushion

This is a beautiful shot that looks much harder to play than it actually is. If you haven't tried the short jenny before, you will probably be amazed at how quickly you can make progress with this shot.

The name *jenny* comes from a thread-spinning device, invented by James Hargreaves in 1764. The term was adopted by billiard players to describe two main shots that require a generous amount of spin—*short*

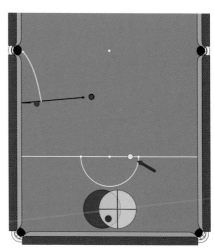

jennies, being in-offs played at acute angles into a middle pocket, and *long* jennies, being played near the side cushion to spin into a top pocket.

It is not usually a good idea to leave yourself a short jenny deliberately but the shot generally comes up after a positional slip-up, such as a middle-pocket loser when the object ball is directed too near to the side cushion.

The short jenny makes use of the effect of the nap on a spinning ball. The spin curves the ball into the middle pocket, making the shot far easier than it would be if it were played without spin. Also, if the cue ball hits the far jaw the spin can help it enter the pocket.

Having a good quality stroke is essential for many shots in billiards and this is especially true for the short jenny. To impart sufficient sidespin it is essential to deliver the cue smoothly through the cue ball with a good follow-through. One of the key cue skills required in billiards is the ability to apply sidespin when playing at a slow to medium pace. Practise a smooth cue delivery and feel your tip bite into the cue ball. Do not be hesitant about addressing near to the edge of the cue ball because if you miscue this will tell you the outer limit that you can address. You will need to experiment with addresses that are close to this limit point so that you can apply maximum sidespin.

As shown in the previous diagram, set the cue ball two-thirds of the way from the middle spot to the end spot of the **D**, with the red 7½ inches (19 cm) from the side cushion and 21 inches (53.3 cm) from the baulk line. Address at 7:30 and aim for a thick half-ball. On some cloths you will find that it is easy to stun the shot accidentally, so if this is the case set the cue ball further away in the **D** (at the same angle).

Now move the object ball to a new position that is reasonably close to the first one and set the cue ball yourself. It is particularly important to set the cue ball accurately in the **D**, and after first setting for the natural angle you will need to narrow that position by moving it by about one ball-width to allow for the reduced throw and the effect of the nap. The exact distance to move the cue ball will vary according to the type and condition of the cloth, so take care to make small adjustments until you are satisfied that the angle you have set is correct.

> **In case you were wondering…**
>
> From some positions it is possible to play very gently to leave another short jenny, but this is not desirable as scoring off a middle-pocket loser is always more certain than off a short jenny.

When the object ball is reasonably close to the pocket the jenny should be played crisply, as you do not want the sidespin to cause the cue ball to drift significantly *before* it reaches the object ball. Start from a position with the red 28½ inches (72.4 cm) from the baulk line and one ball-width away from the side cushion, with the cue ball on the end spot of the **D**. Aim for a *true* half-ball, because you want the cue ball to get away from the red and avoid the double kiss.

Lesson One

The short jenny becomes more challenging as the object ball gets closer to the side cushion and further away from the pocket. Nevertheless, on tables with a good nap it is possible to make the shot from very acute angles. In general, the heavier the cloth the easier the shot will be as the cue ball will curve more as it travels towards the pocket.

Set the red 7 inches (17.8 cm) from the side cushion and 15 inches (38.1 cm) from the baulk line, with the cue ball two-thirds of the way from the middle spot to the end spot of the **D**. At these very acute angles the jenny must be played at a slow pace to allow the nap to curve the cue ball. The contact can be taken slightly thicker than the thick half-ball, to take the pace out of the cue ball and allow the nap to work on the shot.

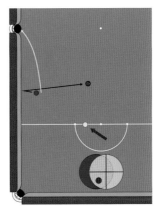

> ### In case you were wondering…
>
> A very advanced technique for playing tight short jennies is to raise the cue butt slightly, applying a slight swerve to the cue ball.

It is worth noting that whenever you are learning new shots, particularly ones which require accurate setting of the cue ball, you might need to repeat them many times to gain confidence. Psychologically it is always best to finish with a successful shot.

Remember
✓ Take your time to set the cue ball accurately
✓ Address at 7:30
✓ Follow through smoothly and apply plenty of sidespin
✓ Play standard short jennies with a thick half-ball contact and at a medium pace
✓ If the object ball is close to the pocket, play crisply at a true half-ball
✓ If the object ball is far from the pocket, play slowly with a thick contact

Concept: Squirt

Squirt is the initial cue ball deflection caused by the off-centre striking required when applying sidespin. It is sometimes called *push-off*. When right side is imparted, the cue ball will push away to the left, and vice versa.

You can prove this to yourself by placing the cue ball tight on the top or bottom cushion and playing with *cushion* side (sometimes referred to as *pocket* side), which is sidespin that helps the cue ball into the pocket after hitting the far jaw. Play at a fast pace, ensuring that your cue is *parallel* to the cushion. Even though the 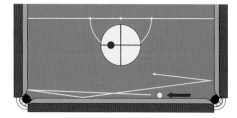 cushion sidespin would help the ball into the pocket if it hit the jaws, you will find that the cue ball squirts sufficiently away from the cushion to miss the pocket.

Squirt is the reason why, when applying sidespin the cue must *not* be parallel to the intended cue ball direction. You must allow for the squirt and aim at a slight angle. If you repeat the previous shot with your cue pointing slightly inwards towards the cushion, it will be a simple matter to drive the cue ball into the corner pocket.

When applying sidespin allow for squirt by aiming at a slight angle

In the example, since left sidespin is applied, the section of the cue at the tip end is pushed to the left as the cue drives through the shot. Since the tip end of the cue initially goes to the left, the ball must go to the right.

The heavier the tip end of the cue, the more the cue ball will squirt. In practical terms, each cue has a different feel and generates a different amount of squirt. Some cues are even manufactured to minimize the mass in the tip end of the cue in order to reduce squirt.

Concept: Swerve

If sidespin is applied with a horizontal cue, and ignoring nap effects, after the initial squirt of the cue ball it will continue on that straight path. However, practically speaking, due to the height of the cushions, most shots are played with the cue pointing slightly downwards. Because of this, after the squirt and subsequent early motion along a straight path, the cue ball will, at some point, turn for a brief moment before once again following a straight path. This is *swerve*.

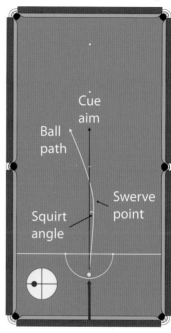

In the diagram the cue is pointing along the spots but initially the cue ball will squirt to the right of the spots. At the swerve point the path changes direction and the cue ball swerves to the left of the spots.

The swerve point is dependent on the speed of the stroke and the friction between the ball and the cloth, assuming the same cue elevation. For example, a fast stroke on a worn cloth would swerve late. The amount of swerve (the angle that the ball takes) is only dependent on the elevation of the cue. If the cue were perfectly level, in other words if there were no cushion rails on the table, there would be no swerve at all.

Cue drill: Swerve

Swerve can be used to make a shot that is otherwise not on, or a low percentage shot that would be very risky if played without swerve. It can also be used for positional purposes. To control swerve shots accurately you need to be fairly close to the first object ball.

Set the balls as shown so that this thin cannon is difficult to make. Try playing the cannon a few times; the position should be such that you miss the cannon more often than not. You might consider *marking the shadows* of

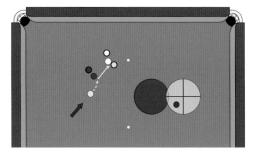

the balls so that you can replace them exactly into their original positions. Now play the cannon with check side, in this case left side. It is not necessary to raise the butt of your cue much. After some practice, you should find that the cannon is much easier when played with check side and you should be able to make it more often than not. These shots should be played at a slow pace, but more speed will be needed as the gap between the cue ball and the red increases. Although you can get an enhanced effect by raising the butt of your cue further, to hit down on the cue ball, this is too difficult to judge at anything but very short distances between the cue ball and the red.

Here, you can get an apparently thicker contact by using running side. For positional purposes, this delicate swerve shot enables you to leave an easy pot red. If you were to play the thin cannon without sidespin you

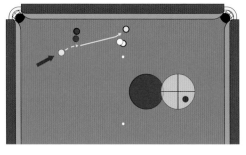

would have to play the shot at around quarter-ball, probably leaving the red on the cushion. Therefore, although a swerve shot such as this, using running side, is less common than the check side swerve, it is worth having in your repertoire.

The Long Jenny

A spinning loser into a top pocket, played along the side cushion, when the object ball is below the middle pocket

This is an attractive shot that looks incredibly difficult but is reasonably straightforward on a cloth with a decent nap. Don't be worried if your shot success rate is low at first as it will take time to learn the required technique, but once you gain confidence you should quickly improve. Once you become accomplished at long jennies you will find that they are tremendously satisfying shots to play. They look fantastic yet top players hardly ever miss them.

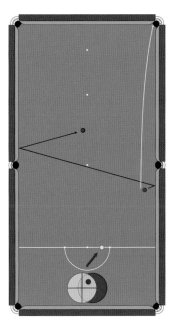

The more sidespin you apply the easier the shot becomes, so it is important to stroke smoothly through the cue ball with a good follow-through. The spin will cause the cue ball to drift towards the side cushion and has the added effect of helping it into the pocket should it hit the top jaw, effectively widening the pocket.

The shot is easier to play at a slower pace because the pocket is more likely to accept the spinning cue ball. Aim for a thick half-ball as thinner contacts will cause the cue ball to travel too quickly after contact with the red. A slightly thicker contact than the thick half-ball will slow down the pace of the cue ball even more, allowing the nap to work more on it, but in this case you will not have much latitude with the contact. Although this is a technique that top players employ, aim for a thick half-ball until you become familiar with the shot.

Lesson One

Set the balls as shown, with the red two ball-widths away from the side cushion and 12 inches (30.5 cm) from an imaginary line across the centre of the table. Put the cue ball on the baulk line, about two-thirds of the way from the middle spot to the end spot of the **D**. Address at 2 o'clock and concentrate on getting the side on, while hitting a thick half-ball. Above-centre striking is normally required to ensure that the cue ball is not skidding on impact. Although you can also make the shot by addressing at 3 o'clock, you will get more squirt by playing the shot this way, making it more difficult to judge. You might choose to set the cue ball slightly further back in the **D** (at the same angle) in order to give more distance from the object ball. This will help to ensure that the cue ball is not skidding by the time it reaches the object ball and it also makes it slightly easier to judge the setting angle.

> **In case you were wondering…**
>
> It is easiest to judge the natural angle when the distance from the cue ball to the object ball is equal to the distance from the object ball to the target.

Remember that the pace of the shot should not be too fast, because you must allow the nap to work on the spinning ball. Push your cue smoothly through the cue ball, using a light grip.

Once you are comfortable with the basic shot, you can try aiming slightly thicker; when you do this you will probably need to tighten the setting angle slightly, moving the cue ball about half a ball-width further to the right. The thicker contact will cause the cue ball to travel more slowly to the pocket.

You can also practise adjusting the strength of the shot, for positional purposes, to bring the red across the table and off the opposite side cushion above the middle pocket, as shown in the diagram. For these faster paced shots you will need to move the cue ball slightly nearer to the middle spot of the **D**. It is normally best to leave an in-off into one of the top pockets but, if the other object ball is situated nicely, you might be able to play the long jenny at a slower pace in order to leave a cannon. Remember that, in general, long jennies are easier to make the slower you play them.

Lesson One

After you are confident with this basic jenny, move the object ball to a new position fairly close to the first one and position the cue ball yourself. Set the cue ball for the thick half-ball loser but then narrow the angle by moving it about one ball-width towards the side cushion. Depending on the table conditions, this setting angle will need to be adjusted to allow for the nap on that particular table, as the stronger the nap, the more the cue ball will drift towards the side cushion.

You might find it surprising that, within reason, the long jenny becomes easier as the object ball gets closer to the side cushion. This is because the cue ball path to the top pocket will be nearly parallel to the cushion and you therefore don't have to judge how much the side will cause it to drift as it travels to the pocket. In this case it is a matter of getting plenty of side on and letting the cue ball spin along the cushion. However, when the object ball is well away from the cushion it is critical that you judge the pace correctly in order to achieve the correct cue ball trajectory. If played with too much pace the cue ball will not curve enough and will hit the top cushion, and if played too slowly it will drift too much and hit the side cushion.

You will find that the nap has an enormous influence on this shot. On a table with a good nap and with the object ball near to the side cushion the long jenny will be relatively straightforward because the cue ball will hug the cushion. However, the same shot on a shaved or worn cloth is much more difficult because the side barely reacts on the nap.

Remember
✓ Make a thick contact
✓ Address at 2 o'clock
✓ Follow through smoothly and apply plenty of sidespin
✓ Bring the object ball away from the opposite side cushion

Try to avoid
✗ Playing the shot with too much pace

Patterns of play: Adapting known shots

Your shot selection and methods of break-building will depend on many things such as your cue skills, knowledge and your preferred patterns of play. As you progress you will learn how small patterns of play can be linked together to form sizeable breaks. Always be on the lookout for adapting shots that you already know, in order to fit the various positional situations that occur during a game.

You have just learned all about the long jenny, and the pattern shown here is a good example of how you can use your long jenny skills to considerable advantage. First of all, from this red middle-pocket loser position, ask yourself where you would like the red to be in order to recover the white, which is in the long jenny position. Although you might be confident with long jennies and feel that the white long jenny is a good option, no matter how good you are at these jennies they will never be certain. If you have a chance to make a cannon, this is almost always a better option than a long jenny, particularly on really tight match tables.

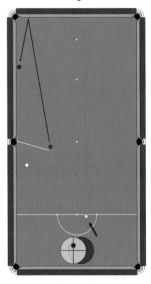

With the white as shown and the red positioned for a middle-pocket loser, most club players would bring the red back to the white and this may well be your preferred pattern of play. A less obvious shot though, is to play the middle-pocket loser to leave the red near the side cushion, on the same side as the white. This is a more advanced pattern of play, especially as it is not obvious at first sight. Once the red is in position, you can play a long jenny *style* cannon, although there is no need to use much sidespin, just a small amount of check side. With practice, you should be able to make the cannon and leave a scoring shot off the red most of the time.

There's one other point that is worth noting from this example of a set pattern—it is important to make a decision to control either *one* or

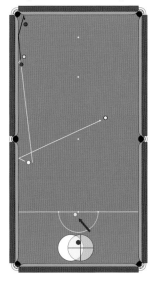

both of the object balls. With the cannon shown here, if you try to do too much with the white, taking it off both side cushions, you are likely to hit the red too hard. In this case, it is much better to forget the white and give full attention to leaving the red in a good position.

If you reverse the positions of the red and the white, so that you have a similar long jenny style cannon from red to white, you will need to adjust the pattern of play accordingly. You can never be sure that you will leave a white *loser* after this cannon, so your attention should be on leaving a good

position off the red, near the opposite middle pocket. To achieve this, the red needs to be taken thinner than the previous shot, at about a true half-ball. If the white is reasonably close to the side cushion, you might find it a slight advantage to hit the cushion before the white, as this is more likely to leave an in-off white. Controlling the position of the balls after this cannon is not so easy, making this shot more risky than the white to red cannon. For this reason it is best not to play for this position, but all the same, it is a shot you should be familiar with.

Concept: Drag

A *drag* shot is when the cue ball starts off rotating backwards but begins rolling *before* contacting the object ball. If you strike the cue ball well below centre you will cause it to rotate backwards as it travels forwards. Cloth friction will eventually convert this motion into a roll and if this happens before the cue ball hits the object ball you will have played a drag shot.

Drag, when *combined* with side, helps the cue ball retain as much sidespin as possible. You have already played one shot that makes use of drag—the short jenny. Once the drag wears off it is almost as if the sidespin is released. Also, by using drag you can actually get more sidespin on the cue ball, mainly because the below centre striking will require you to strike it harder.

> **In case you were wondering…**
>
> It is easy to see the point at which the backspin changes to roll as the forward motion of the cue ball appears to slow before this point and speed up after it.

Drag helps to deliver maximum sidespin to the object ball

> **In case you were wondering…**
>
> A shot played with drag *and* side causes the axis of rotation (due to the sidespin) to flip just as the backspin changes to roll.

Another effect of using drag combined with side is that the nap will not cause a fast-moving spinning cue ball to drift significantly *before* making contact with the object ball. This makes spinning drag shots easier to judge than those played with spin alone.

Finally, drag shots *without* spin are less likely to roll off due to the faster pace required and can be easier to judge than naturally rolling shots.

Drag limits the nap effect and reduces the chance of a roll-off

Cue drill: Drag

This pot, played to leave the cue ball in position for a middle cross-loser, is a good example of a shot that should be played with drag. Address at 4:30 to get plenty of side on the cue ball, playing the shot firmly, so that it runs off the side cushion and into position. Playing with drag preserves the sidespin and allows you to hit the cue ball firmly. It would be much more difficult to achieve the same positional outcome if you addressed above centre.

Although this next pot red is easy to make, it should always be played with drag. A naturally rolling pot would have to be played exceptionally slowly, in order to leave the cue ball in position for a middle cross-loser. This type of slow shot often goes wrong as it is very common for the cue ball to roll off by a small amount, perhaps contacting the red too thinly and leaving the cue ball on the side cushion.

Play the pot crisply, with drag and sidespin. This minimizes the chance of a roll-off and, after contact, the right sidespin will curl the cue ball away from the side cushion and along a line for the middle cross-loser. These subtle but beneficial changes in how seemingly simple shots are played can make a significant difference to your match-winning potential.

Lesson One

For this shot, use drag without any sidespin to limit any roll-off that the table might have. Also, for long-distance shots such as this, you will find it much easier to control the pace of the object ball by using drag.

This next diagram shows an awkward position but the thin cannon is slightly easier to make than the run-through as long as you play it crisply using drag combined with check side. The drag limits any roll-off and preserves the

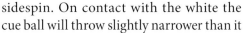

sidespin. On contact with the white the cue ball will throw slightly narrower than it would do without spin, making the shot more certain. There is a slight swerve effect, due to the sidespin, which also helps to make the cannon. If you attempted to play this thin cannon with a slow naturally rolling shot, you would have very little chance of making it.

In case you were wondering…

For a shot played with drag, at the moment the cue ball starts rolling it will be travelling at about 70% of its initial speed.

The Long-range Jenny

A spinning loser into a top pocket, played along the side cushion, when the object ball is above the middle pocket

When the object ball is past the middle pocket and close to the side cushion, it is possible to play a spinning loser into the top pocket. This shot is often referred to simply as the *long jenny*, but as it is played quite differently from that shot it is referred to here as the *long-range jenny*.

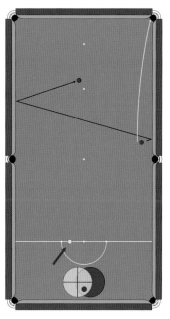

Set the cue ball about two-thirds of the way from the middle spot to the end spot of the **D**, with the red 8 inches (20.3 cm) from an imaginary line across the centre of the table and two ball-widths off the side cushion. Address at 4:30, pushing smoothly through the cue ball to apply maximum sidespin. Play at a slightly faster pace than the standard long jenny, otherwise the side will grip too much on the nap, causing the cue ball to curve too much *before* reaching the red. Aim for a thick half-ball but avoid getting too thick a contact because this can cause a double kiss.

The object ball should be taken off the opposite side cushion to finish as shown in the diagram. Of course you might wish to adjust the pace of the shot, depending on the position of the second object ball.

After you are confident with this shot, move the red to a new position fairly close to the first one and set the cue ball yourself. As with other jennies, remember to narrow the angle to allow for the check side and the effect of the nap. Start off by narrowing the natural angle by about a ball-width, adjusting the setting angle depending on the table conditions.

You will find that when the red is very near the side cushion it is easy to miss the shot by getting a double kiss. These jennies are quite a challenge and you will need to play a thinner contact, at least as thin as a true half-ball, to avoid this double kiss.

If the red is further away from the side cushion, so that the shot is only *just* possible, even with the cue ball at the edge of the **D**, you can contact the red slightly thicker than the thick half-ball to narrow the throw marginally and also to slow the cue ball down. The nap will then have more time to work on the spinning ball as it travels towards the pocket, curving it towards the side cushion.

Remember
✓ Address at 4:30
✓ Follow through smoothly to apply maximum sidespin
✓ When the object ball is very close to the side cushion, aim thinner than the thick half-ball
✓ When the angle is tight, aim thicker than the thick half-ball
✓ Bring the object ball away from the side cushions

Try to avoid
✗ The double kiss

The Tight Loser *with* the Nap
An in-off into a top pocket, taking advantage of various aspects of using sidespin

This shot comes up regularly and is interesting as it takes advantage of four different aspects of applying sidespin.

Firstly, the shot is played with drag, in order to preserve as much sidespin as possible. Secondly, since the shot is played with the nap, the cue ball will drift to the same side as the applied sidespin. This has to be taken into account by aiming for a thinner contact than is actually required. On contact with the object ball, the cue ball deflection angle will be reduced due to the throw effect of the spinning ball, further narrowing the angle. Finally, approaching the pocket, the still spinning cue ball effectively widens the pocket.

It is essential that you get plenty of sidespin on the cue ball and that you push your cue right through the shot with a long follow-through. Set the white slightly too tight for a standard thick half-ball loser from hand. Once you can make that shot using plenty of drag and sidespin, tighten it slightly further by moving the white nearer to the side cushion. The aim point will depend on the table conditions and you will have to allow for the nap effect.

Remember
✓ Apply a generous amount of sidespin
✓ Adjust your aim to compensate for the nap effect

Lesson One

Shot selection: A choice of in-offs

With this position you have the choice of a short jenny off the red or a long-range loser off the white. In most cases, you should be able to make a decision on which shot to play within a few seconds, as you will probably have seen a similar position during a previous game.

Here, there are several factors that should influence your decision to play the in-off white rather than the jenny. Firstly, the jenny is a lower percentage shot than the in-off white and, should you miss the jenny, you are likely to leave an easy opening for your opponent. An even more important point is that the jenny has no significant purpose because the white is in an awkward position for you to eventually leave a cannon. The only decent position in which to leave the red would be within a small area on the right side of the table, near the side cushion and above the pyramid spot. As this is difficult

to achieve, you will almost certainly end up playing the in-off white and, having played the jenny first, there is a good chance that you might knock the white onto the red and spoil position!

Most top players would begin with the in-off white, taking the white in and out of baulk slightly to the left of the spots. They would look to follow this with either a cannon from white to red, a white middle-pocket loser or, if the long-range loser was played too hard for either of these shots, the red jenny.

Here, playing from hand, there is a choice of a long-range jenny off the white or a short jenny off the red. If you play the white jenny, you will probably hope to leave a white loser in order to then bring the white around to the red. Alternatively, you could play a similar jenny to leave the white somewhere near to the billiard spot before playing the red short jenny. Both of these patterns have risks; you might get out of position or miss a shot.

If you play the red jenny first, you will probably look to leave a red middle-pocket loser. From this position, you could push the red towards the top cushion, leaving a drop cannon from white to red. You might miss the jenny, so there is a small risk there, and of course you are likely to leave your opponent in if you do so. You might make the red jenny but find that you get an awkward leave from the drop cannon, as drop cannons are easy to score from but never certain to leave perfect position. But if it all goes to plan you will end up at the top of the table, which will be a nice reward for your efforts.

This last position is quite awkward as it is extremely easy to play the white loser and mistakenly pot the white at the same time. You

should never take this risk, but play the in-off white in such a way as to avoid the four-shot. Having just learnt how to play tight losers with the nap, you might decide to *tighten* the setting angle slightly and play with check side to take the white off the top cushion. However, if the white were slightly

> **In case you were wondering…**
>
> A four-shot, with the white and yellow disappearing into separate top pockets is sometimes called a *pair of breeches*!

nearer the **D** it might be better to *widen* the angle slightly and play with running side, to take the white off the side cushion. You might also choose to play this shot fractionally thinner than normal, to cut the white to the side cushion. Experiment with different white positions and make sure that you can control the white's path.

The Drifting Long Loser

An in-off into a top pocket which takes advantage of the nap effect when using sidespin

Occasionally, you will be faced with positions allowing you to use either running or check side to work with the nap, causing the cue ball to drift slowly towards a corner pocket.

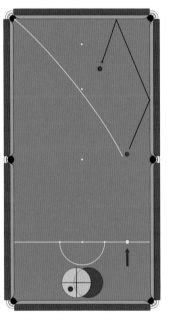

Even though this red loser could be played using a fast pace, by playing a forcer, you would probably cause the red to end up in baulk. There is a better way to play the shot. By playing with running side the cue ball will initially throw wider on contact with the red and then drift *with* the nap as it travels towards the corner pocket.

Although only half maximum sidespin would normally be used to play wide losers, it is not appropriate here because *maximum* sidespin will get the best effect out of the nap. The shot needs to be played at a slow pace, so that the nap has sufficient time to work on the spinning ball. Of course, a similar type of shot can be used to make a cannon that is wide, a good example of this being a wide drop cannon.

To practise playing the shot, set the cue ball on the baulk line halfway from the end spot of the **D** to the side cushion and the red one ball-width further up the table than the centre, and the same distance from the side cushion as the cue ball. Before practising this in-off with running side, play it without any side at all to convince yourself that it cannot be made with a naturally rolling shot.

Lesson One

Now play the shot with maximum sidespin, making sure to cue smoothly with a long follow-through. Ensure that the contact is a thick half-ball to get the widest throw and also to limit the pace of the cue ball. If you make a thinner contact than this you are likely to leave the cue ball with too much pace as it travels to the corner pocket, so it will drift less on the nap and you won't make the shot.

When the angle is tight you can use a similar technique, but with check side. The same principles apply and you will need to get maximum sidespin on the cue ball and play at a slow pace, to let the nap curve the ball into the pocket. You can also play a thicker contact, up to three-quarter-ball, in order to narrow the angle even further.

Set the cue ball on the baulk line 21 inches (53.3 cm) from the side cushion and the red in line with the centre spot and the cue ball. From this particular position it is quite difficult to get the red into position for a loser from hand, but you should be able to make the shot quite comfortably and with the white in the position shown it should be a straightforward matter to make a white to red cannon afterwards.

Of course, these wide and narrow drifting long loser positions are often left so that you do not need maximum sidespin to make the shots. In these cases you will have to use your judgement as to how much sidespin to apply.

Remember
✓ For wide shots aim for a thick half-ball
✓ For narrow shots aim for at least as thick as a thick half-ball
✓ Follow through smoothly

Try to avoid
✗ Using too much pace

The Narrow Drop Cannon

A drop cannon, which uses check side to take advantage of the nap effect

The narrow drop cannon is a shot that occurs quite frequently and, providing that the angle is not too narrow, is a good method for getting to the top. However, if the shot is extremely tight and you feel that there is a risk of missing the cannon, play a long loser off the white instead.

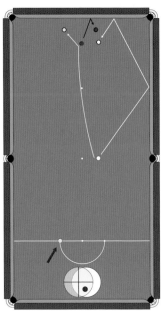

Check side is applied to work *with* the nap to make cannons that are very tight. As always, check side initially narrows the throw but then the spinning cue ball drifts even narrower as it moves with the nap. The shot is best taken thicker than a thick half-ball, as this will cause a narrower throw than the natural angle. Of course, you could get a narrow path by playing a thin contact, but in this case the cue ball would travel too quickly and the nap would not have time to work as effectively on the spinning ball. Consequently, it is difficult to play the cannon this way and much better to play the shot shown.

For ease of setting up the shot, the diagram indicates a cannon played from an end spot of the **D** although, with the white in the position shown, it would normally be considered a better billiards shot to play the long loser. Nevertheless, top players sometimes choose to play this tight cannon rather than the long loser off the white, particularly if they are comfortable with the table conditions and are confident that they can judge how the spinning cue ball will react on the nap.

Lesson One

Practise playing the shot by setting the white 8 inches (20.3 cm) to the side of the centre spot, the red on the billiard spot and the cue ball on the end spot of the **D**. Before playing with sidespin you might want to try a thick half-ball contact, addressing at centre ball, to see by how much the cue ball misses the red.

Now address at 4:30, concentrating on pushing your cue through the shot and, for the moment, making a thick half-ball contact. The cue ball should travel slowly up the table and just reach the red, while the white comes off the side cushion to meet the other two balls. Once you have mastered this, practise making an even thicker contact on the white, as shown in the diagram.

> ### In case you were wondering...
>
> The technique of making the cue ball travel very slowly towards the second object ball in order to only *just* make the cannon (often played with plenty of sidespin) is sometimes referred to as *floating the cue ball.*

Remember
✓ Play at least a thick half-ball
✓ Apply plenty of check side

Try to avoid
✗ Hitting the shot too hard

Lesson One

Concept: Sidespin *against* the nap

Against the nap, a spinning ball drifts the *opposite* way to that which you might expect. *Right* sidespin on the cue ball will cause it to drift *left*, and vice versa. The cue ball will push off line with the initial impact of the tip and then drift in the opposite direction to the sidespin that was imparted.

In the diagram, left side is imparted to the cue ball so that it spins clockwise. As it moves towards the baulk cushion the nap will cause it to drift to the right.

Against the nap, left sidespin causes a ball to drift to the right and vice versa

Another fundamental issue regarding playing with side against the nap is that the cue ball will deviate more *against* the nap than the equivalent shot *with* the nap. You could expect that with a reasonable cloth the cue ball would drift about a full ball-width, using maximum sidespin, at a slow pace, going with the nap along the length of the table. You would expect it to deviate at least an extra third to half a ball-width when going against the nap.

A spinning ball drifts significantly when played *against* the nap

Shots that are narrower or wider than the natural angle are not usually played with sidespin *against* the nap. Against the nap, on contact with the object ball, check side initially does help as it causes the cue ball to *throw narrower* (as it always does). However, after contact, as the cue ball travels against the nap it will *drift wider*, so the two effects more or less cancel each other out and you might as well have played

Lesson One

the shot without sidespin in the first place! For example, you have just seen the narrow drop cannon using check side with the nap, but don't try a similar shot against the nap. Similarly, if you want a ball to drift *wider* when playing against the nap, sidespin is once again best left alone. In summary, avoid using sidespin when trying to adjust the natural angle when playing *against* the nap. For narrow shots it is normally better to adjust the contact and for wide positions to play a forcing shot.

Against the nap, normally avoid using side for shots
narrower or wider than the natural angle

Apart from when the object ball is close to the pocket (when pocket side can be used), shots spinning along a cushion are more difficult when played against the nap as the *wrong* side needs to be used. Cushion (or pocket) side would cause the ball to drift away from the cushion. So, in-offs along a cushion and against the nap have to be played at *exact strength* or the non-pocket side will keep the cue ball out of the pocket.

Also, potting against the nap is more challenging than when playing with the nap, because any unintended sidespin can cause the cue ball to drift significantly. As it is so tricky to judge the effect of sidespin against the nap, when potting against the nap it is almost always best to play without sidespin, as even medium paced shots will drift enough to cause you to miss the pot.

Avoid using side when potting
against the nap

Although you should be wary of using side when playing against the nap, you are about to learn some shots that are only possible by using sidespin to cause the cue ball to drift. It is difficult to judge just how much the sidespin will make the cue ball curve and these types of shot tend to be played when there is no better alternative.

Lesson One

The Jenny *against* the Nap

A spinning loser into a middle pocket, played against the nap, when both balls are near the side cushion

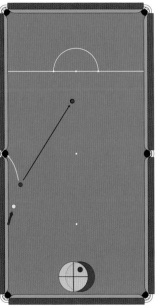

This shot looks impossible but works remarkably well on a table with a decent nap. If the shot is played correctly it is incredible how much the cue ball will curve. This is quite a rare shot, as it is not one that is played for deliberately and the balls need to be left exactly for the correct angle. Nevertheless, it is worth having it in your repertoire.

There are three important points regarding this shot. The first is that you need to get as much side as possible on the cue ball. Secondly, the shot needs to be at a thick contact, around three-quarter-ball. Lastly, the cue ball should only *just* reach the pocket, allowing the nap to work on the spinning cue ball.

By making a thick contact you can be less tentative with your delivery and confidently push through the cue ball, getting plenty of sidespin on, as the thick contact will absorb much of the pace of the cue ball. There is not much margin for error with this shot so it is only worth playing when the distance to the object ball is small. You will need to address high on the cue ball to avoid any unintentional stun.

Set the balls as shown, with the red 12 inches (30.5 cm) from an imaginary line across the centre of the table and 5 inches (12.7 cm) off the side cushion. The cue ball should be off the cushion and in a line such that if you played the red full-ball, it would hit the centre of the baulk cushion. It is quite difficult to set up the position exactly and you might need to adjust it slightly. Bear in mind that the cue ball needs to be reasonably close to the object ball for this shot to work, otherwise the nap will work on the cue ball *before* contact. Also, you should not practise playing this shot on tables with particularly worn or shaved cloths because you will have little success. During your practice, you will have to repeat this shot many times, adjusting contact and pace until you are confident with the outcome. The great thing about it is that you will always leave a middle-pocket loser or a pot red, should you make the shot.

> ### In case you were wondering...
>
> For a given amount of sidespin, the slower a ball is travelling the greater the spin-to-speed ratio and the longer the nap has to affect the cue ball's path.

Remember
✓ Apply plenty of sidespin
✓ Make sure that you make a thick contact
✓ The cue ball should only just reach the pocket

Try to avoid
✗ Too thin a contact

The Tight Loser *against* the Nap
An in-off into a baulk pocket, taking advantage of various aspects of using sidespin

As with the tight loser *with* the nap, this is a shot which takes advantage of four different aspects of applying sidespin.

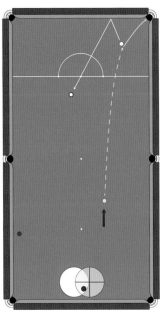

Firstly, the shot is played with drag, in order to preserve as much sidespin as possible before contact with the object ball. As the shot is played against the nap, using left side, the cue ball will drift to the right. This has to be taken into account by aiming for a thicker contact than is actually required. On contact with the object ball, the cue ball deflection angle will be reduced due to the throw effect of the spinning ball. Finally, on reaching the pocket jaws, the still spinning cue ball effectively widens the pocket.

Set up a similar position, slightly too tight for a standard thick half-ball loser. *Aim* for a about a thick half-ball and play at a medium pace. You should see the cue ball drift to the right resulting in a thinner than true half-ball contact on the white. Don't play the shot too slowly because this makes it more difficult to judge the aim point owing to the increased drift. Also, after contact, the cue ball will curve the wrong way and, when the white is further from the pocket than the position shown, this can be significant.

Remember
✓ Apply plenty of sidespin
✓ Adjust your aim to compensate for the nap effect

Concept: Running through

Following through the object ball is more often known as *running through*, although both terms are commonly used. When playing nearly full-ball shots, there are several ways to get the cue ball to run through after contact with the object ball.

The natural roll run-through

The most common method is the *natural roll run-through*. These shots are played smoothly and usually quite slowly, with above centre striking.

It is important to realize that, practically speaking, you will not be able to spin a ball forward faster than it can roll naturally—the best you can do is to get the cue ball rolling naturally *almost* immediately. This occurs with a high tip *contact point*, about halfway from the centre to the top of the ball. If the cue ball is struck anywhere below this it will skid for a while before it starts rolling naturally and this will be more noticeable on fine or new cloths because there is so little friction.

**The natural roll run-through is played
smoothly with a high address**

The forcing run-through

The *forcing run-through* is a reasonably powerful shot, using a high address, to drive through the object ball. These run-throughs are played when the distance from cue ball to object ball is not sufficient for the cue ball to be rolling naturally by the time it reaches the object ball.

On impact with the object ball, there is a brief moment when the cue ball hesitates before it drives forward. At this point, although the cue ball's forward motion has temporarily ceased it continues spinning forwards until frictional effects take over and it once again sets off on a forward path. Of course you don't see any of this happening as it all occurs in an instant, too quick for the eye to notice.

**The forcing run-through is normally played at
a fast pace and with a high address**

Lesson One

The drag run-through

The most advanced type of run-through is the drag run-through, where the cue ball is addressed below centre but stops skidding and begins rolling before hitting the object ball. For these shots you will need to be able to judge that the skid has finished by the time the cue ball impacts the object ball.

**The drag run-through is played by
addressing below centre**

Often, these various types of run-through are used in conjunction with sidespin, either for positional purposes or to make the shot easier, or sometimes both. In fact, the drag run-through is almost always played with sidespin. There is also a fourth type of run-through, the stun run-through, which will be covered in lesson two.

Before embarking on many of these run-throughs, you might find it useful to understand the following rule to help you aim and judge the correct contact point on the object ball.

Concept: The run-through rule

To run through a ball into a pocket, aim for the point where an imaginary ball would touch the object ball, on the far side of it, so that the centres of the object and imaginary balls point to the pocket.

This rule clearly works for run-through cannons as well as run-through losers and is a very good starting point for someone trying to learn these shots as it gives a point of aim. After a while though, you will learn to see the aim point without referring to this rule and most experienced billiard players simply judge the contact, playing the run-through using their knowledge and experience of the shot.

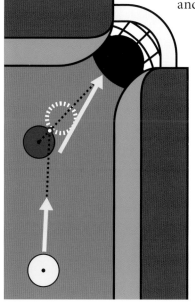

To follow through off the red and make the in-off, aim the centre of the cue ball at the edge of the imaginary ball on the far side of the red, indicated by the small blue circle.

When you are practising, you can help to identify the correct contact point by judging the point between a missed shot on both the thin and the thick sides. If you are missing the shot on one particular side, force yourself to overcompensate so that you miss it on the other side. Gradually work at the shot until you learn the correct point of contact.

Also, when you are starting out with these shots there can be a tendency to aim for too thin a contact on the object ball. Until you become confident with these shots, you will probably find that the object ball must be hit thicker than you think.

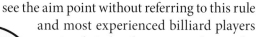

The Run-through Cannon

A run-through, played at a very thick contact off the first object ball, in order to make a cannon

Run-through cannons are an essential part of advanced billiards and there is hardly a break that will be made without one of these shots. There is a huge variety of run-through cannons as any shot thicker than a thick half-ball that causes the cue ball to follow through is technically a run-through. It is best to begin with a natural roll run-through and develop your skills from there.

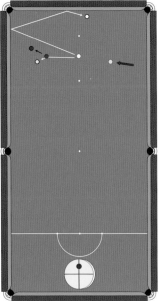

Set the balls as indicated in the diagram, with an angle for the cannon set between a three-quarter and a full-ball shot. Address high on the cue ball and make sure that you cue smoothly so as to get it rolling naturally as soon as possible.

Play the run-through cannon with natural roll on the cue ball. Avoid using sidespin and concentrate on leaving the red in a good position. Make sure that the second ball contact is *not* on the right side of the red. Do not hit the white too hard, as it should finish reasonably close to the spot.

In general, run-throughs are easier to judge the closer to a full-ball contact you can make. For this shot, you might find it difficult to convince yourself that the contact should be nearly full-ball. Bear in mind that it is common to miss these run-throughs on the thin side.

Although this cannon can be made with a natural roll run-through, a forcing run-through cannon should be played in order to take the red off two cushions and leave it near the left middle pocket. A bonus of the shot is that the white can be contacted fully to nudge it off the side cushion. With these faster paced run-throughs, if you don't hit the first object ball thick enough you will miss the cannon by quite a margin, so it is better for any contact error to be on the thick side.

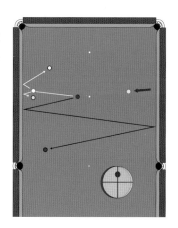

This cannon is also played using a forcing run-through. Play the shot with plenty of power and address well above centre, with no sidespin. You don't have to set the position up exactly as shown as any similar position will suffice.

It is worth practising this type of shot from different positions. You might find it surprising how easy it is to make these run-through cannons, even over large distances, although the positional aspect is never certain.

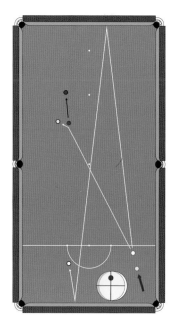

Remember
✓ The required contact is often thicker than you might think
✓ With forcing run-throughs, contact errors on the *thin side* will cause you to miss by a large amount

Try to avoid
✗ Applying sidespin when playing forcing run-throughs

Cue drill: Second ball contact

One of the most valuable skills in billiards is to be able to make an accurate contact on the *second* object ball. This is achieved mainly by varying the contact on the *first* object ball, although you might also adjust the address and the pace of the shot.

Set the balls as shown, with the red in line from the centre of the pocket to the middle spot of the **D** and about two ball-widths from the drop of the pocket (so that you could fit two balls between the red and the pocket). Set the white about 7 inches (18 cm) from the side cushion and 7 inches (18 cm) from the red. The cue ball should be level with the white and about 7 inches (18 cm) from it. From this position play a thick run-through cannon to pot the red and make a *five-shot*.

Once you have mastered this, bring the cue ball a little nearer to the side cushion (perpendicular

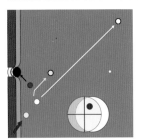

to the original position) and try the five-shot from this different angle. Initially, don't use any sidespin, but once you are comfortable with the shot, introduce some check side to throw the red towards the pocket. Continue this routine until the cue ball is on the side cushion. At this position, you will need to make a thick half-ball contact and use some running side, to pot the red.

Once you have mastered these run-throughs you might want to try some thin cannons, similar to the one shown here. Of course, you can also set up many similar practice positions of your own choosing. Experiment by varying the thickness of contact on the white and by adjusting the amount of sidespin applied.

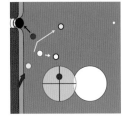

Concept: Using check side with run-throughs

For slow and medium paced run-throughs, sidespin will help the cue ball to run through the object ball. The application of check side is a particularly useful technique if you need to run through and limit the movement of the first object ball. However, if there is a large distance between the two object balls, it is usually advisable to avoid using any sidespin, as the nap can cause the cue ball to drift significantly.

**Consider using check side to facilitate a thick run-through
but only when the balls are reasonably close together**

Cue drill: Using check side with run-throughs

This is the type of shot that requires check side to limit the pace of the first object ball. Set the balls approximately as shown, marking their shadows so that you can replace them accurately, and play the run-through cannon with above centre striking. Don't use any sidespin and see how gently you can play the cannon. Then play the cannon with plenty of check side, addressing at 1:30 as shown in the diagram.

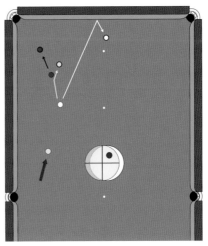

You will find that it is much easier to limit the pace of the white when using check side. This is a good example of a shot where accurate second ball contact is extremely important.

Cue drill: Running through using drag and sidespin

Place the red level with the pyramid spot and the cue ball level with the billiard spot. Play the following four run-throughs, in sequence, all at a strength so that the red finishes close to the bottom cushion.

You might find it surprising to see that the first shot, played without sidespin, gives the shortest run-through. The next shot, played with *running side*, gives a significant improvement. The third shot, played with *check side*, is even better. Now play the shot at position 4, addressing at 7:30. Cue smoothly to run through and try to avoid stabbing at the cue ball. Concentrate on making a distinct *push* of the cue with a large follow-through, letting the weight of the cue itself generate the required sidespin. With practice, you should get a slightly better result than the previous shot and be able to get the cue ball to reach at least halfway to the centre spot.

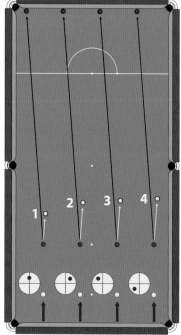

Using a low address helps to apply maximum sidespin, which makes the cue ball follow through incredibly easily—even though below centre striking *without* sidespin would be useless! However, you might find this drill quite a challenge and if you do find difficulty running through with drag, even after a good amount of practice, it will probably be best to play run-throughs by addressing above centre. Do not be concerned about this as many accomplished billiard players play all run-throughs this way. Remember that the more sidespin you can impart, the easier the cue ball will run through, so don't be hesitant about experimenting with the limits of your cue ball address. A spotted cue ball will help you to see the spin.

Lesson One

The Cushion Run-through
A spinning run-through loser played along the cushion into a corner pocket

This shot occurs quite frequently and is certainly one that needs to be mastered to improve your match-winning potential.

It is best to address below centre, in order to impart the maximum amount of sidespin, something that significantly assists the shot. Remember that, when addressing below centre, by the time the cue ball reaches the object ball it should have

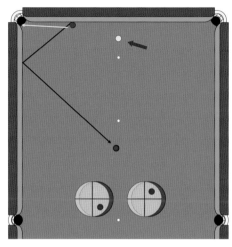

Lesson One

stopped skidding but will still carry the sidespin. However, at close distances, and on some tables with responsive cloths, addressing below centre can be risky as the cue ball can still be skidding on contact, resulting in an unintentional stun shot.

If you have difficulty with this shot, address above centre until you become more confident at achieving a run-through when addressing below centre. Remember that punchy or jerky cue actions will cause the cue ball to stun off the red.

Set the balls for a cushion run-through, with the red on the top cushion halfway from the spot to the pocket and the cue ball halfway from the spot to the top cushion. Cue smoothly, using either of the addresses shown in the diagram. The object ball should come off the side cushion, leaving a loser from hand. If the cue ball is not following through, your cue action probably needs some adjustment so try to push the cue ball rather than strike it. It is the quality of your stroke that is important and you need to be able to impart the sidespin without stunning the cue ball. Don't worry if you can only make the shot by addressing above centre; although you won't get maximum sidespin on the cue ball you can still learn to make the shot consistently.

Also, when you are starting out with these shots there can be a tendency to aim for too thin a contact on the object ball, so until you become confident with them you will probably find that the object ball must be hit thicker than you think.

More often than not, the object ball will be slightly away from the cushion. Therefore, after you are confident with the basic shot, move the red off the top cushion by about half a ball-width and practise running through from this position.

It is also worth practising run-throughs when the object ball is close to the cue ball. At close range, you will definitely need to make sure that you use a high address on the cue ball, otherwise you will stun the shot. As a guide, if the cue ball is less than about 18 inches (46 cm) from the object ball, you will probably be better off addressing above centre, to avoid unintentional stun.

A good practice routine is to play run-throughs off the white when it is near the top cushion and the red is on the spot. Ideally, you should leave a drop cannon but you might leave an in-off white, in which case you will have to play another in-off before the drop cannon. If, during a match, you were unsure of the table conditions, it would be best to avoid playing directly for the drop cannon as you might leave the white very close to the side cushion. It is always a safer option to leave the white centrally placed for an in-off.

Remember
✓ If you can, address below centre to apply maximum sidespin
✓ Push your cue smoothly through the cue ball

Try to avoid
✗ Hitting the object ball too thin

Concept: Avoiding the double kiss

There are occasions on fairly straight run-throughs when the object ball will tangle with the pocket and get in the way of the cue ball as it travels towards the pocket. In these cases you should assess whether the run-through can be made. If the object ball is the red it is normally a better, and less risky, option to play the pot. Otherwise, there are several methods that you can employ to avoid the double kiss. Make sure that you experiment with the following shots.

Cue drill: Avoiding the double kiss

The jaw method

Probably the easiest way of avoiding the double kiss is to get the object ball to *jaw* and then move away from the pocket. Success at this method will depend on the pocket size and jaw shape.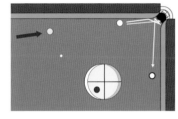

Of course, a middle pocket jaw can also be helpful to avoid potting the white, or getting a double kiss, when attempting an in-off into a middle pocket. In this case, right side is used to throw the white to the left so that it hits the middle pocket jaw. This clears the path for the cue ball to follow through into the pocket.

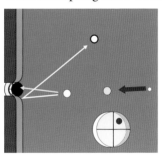

Jaw the object ball to clear a path to the pocket

The side method

You can control the path of the object
ball slightly by adjusting the amount
of sidespin. Remember that check side
will straighten the path of the object
ball. It is worth experimenting with
various positions. It is even possible
to play with the *wrong* side, as shown,
to get the object ball away from the

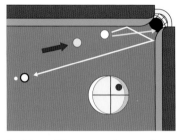

possible double kiss, although this probably will not work on ultra-
tight match tables as the pocket will not accept the cue ball. Even on
tables with generous pockets, shots played with the wrong side should
only be played when the object ball is close to the pocket.

**Adjust the amount of sidespin
to avoid the double kiss**

The stun method

If the object ball is close to the pocket
it is possible to address only slightly
above centre and to use a faster pace
to get the object ball out of the way.
The fast pace of the shot drives the
object ball into the cushion rubber
and out at a sharper angle. You will
learn much more about stun shots in
the next lesson.

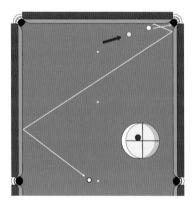

**A stun shot can force the object ball
out of the way of the double kiss**

The bounce-along method

At wide angles the cushion run-through is simply not on, because you will get the double kiss immediately as the object ball comes off the cushion. However, the run-through *is* still possible but only by playing a very advanced shot. The in-off needs to be played with a lot of pace and a high address; the object ball then gets out of the way of the cue ball because the cue ball pauses at the initial impact before driving forward again. Applying some check side will help to make the in-off. The fast pace drives the object ball into the cushion, whilst the cue ball hesitates and then moves forwards again. The object ball is able to get out of the way and the cue ball arcs into the pocket, sometimes bouncing off the cushion several times in the process. You probably won't have much success with this shot as it is challenging, even for very advanced players, but it is fun to have a go to see if you can make it. You might be surprised to find that the same bounce-along run-through works equally well into a baulk pocket.

> ### In case you were wondering…
>
> There is an even more advanced version of this shot when the object ball is tight on the side cushion about 8 inches (20 cm) below the middle pocket and the cue ball is in hand. A bounce-along loser can be played into the middle pocket, but this is not really practical, simply more of an exhibition shot.

The bounce-along run-through can be used to avoid the double kiss

Lesson One

The Running Side Run-through
An in-off played with running side to run through and spin the cue ball into a blind pocket

This is a fantastic match-winning shot that is often overlooked. It is quite an easy shot, as long as you apply plenty of sidespin. Shot success depends on getting as much side as possible on the cue ball and avoiding any stun.

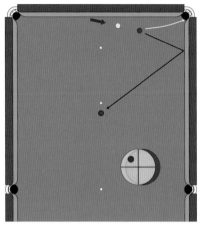

Set the balls as shown in the diagram, with the red halfway from the spot to both the side and top cushions and the cue ball about one ball-width off the top cushion and about 9 inches (23 cm) from the red. Play the shot with a smooth cue action and, as the balls are close together, make sure to address above centre.

When you are comfortable with the shot, move the balls further from the pocket, keeping the same distance from the cue ball to the red. Provided you make a good contact, as long as you apply sufficient sidespin the cue ball will spin into the pocket. These shots become more challenging the further away the cue ball is from the red, because it is difficult to make an accurate contact.

Remember
✓ Apply plenty of sidespin
✓ Push your cue smoothly through the cue ball

Try to avoid
✗ Stunning the cue ball

Patterns of play: Running side run-through cannon

When you are practising, it is often a good idea to start from set positions that are quite challenging, rather than simply setting up the balls in prime position. Then, when you come across similar positions in a match, you will be confident with your pattern of play. Here is another pattern of play that can be adapted from a shot you know.

This is a good position from which to start your practice as you will have several shots to play before you manage to get the balls in prime position, and these little challenges can be fun and a great way to improve your break-building.

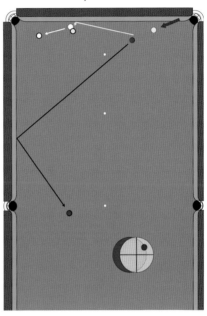

The run-through cannon is a useful shot, with the white being a big target because it is so close to the cushion. Although you could play a thin cannon, you would be unlikely to leave a good positional outcome by playing the shot that way. The best way to play this shot is to play it as a run-through cannon, with the running side that you would use if you were playing an in-off. If you play this cannon with check side the white is likely to roll along the top cushion towards the pocket. However, running side helps to keep the cue ball close to the top cushion and to nudge the white off it. By playing the shot at around three-quarter-ball you should push the red near the position shown and leave an in-off white. You should be able to make the cannon successfully on most occasions and, from a seemingly awkward leave, you can develop both object balls into prime position.

Shot selection: Leaving both balls in prime position

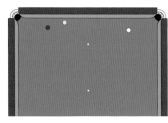

Here, there is the opportunity of a running side run-through loser off either the red or the white, or possibly even a pot red.

You can see that the distance from the cue ball to the white is large enough to make this run-through a risky shot, even though the white is reasonably close to the pocket. Of course it might be worth considering the pot white, especially if you only need a few points for game. On the other hand the pot red might be your choice of shot, although it wouldn't be the best option if you were comfortable with the running side run-through that you learned in this lesson. Most top players would play this run-through loser off the red to leave both object balls in good scoring positions, especially as the white is already in a reasonable position for an in-off from hand.

This next position seems straightforward, but you have a choice of several shots. The pot red is easy to make and it is a relatively simple matter to leave a middle cross-loser or to get to the spot end for a pot. It is worth noting that positioning for two pots off the spot is usually a poor pattern of play, so a middle cross-loser is a better positional option from this pot red. A run-through in-off red could be played, probably with some left sidespin to ensure that the red misses the pocket jaw and to push it near to the pyramid spot. An important point though, is that

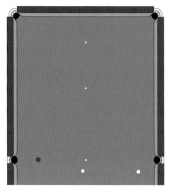

if you play off the red (with either a pot or an in-off) the white is in a poor position when playing from hand and so the best shot would be to play a run-through off the white to leave it positioned for a middle-pocket loser. The red is already positioned for a loser from hand, so by taking the in-off white you will have control of both object balls.

The Three-quarter-ball Loser

A three-quarter-ball run-through into a middle pocket to leave a similar shot

This run-through loser is one that can be used very effectively to make sequences of middle-pocket losers, but in match play it is not one for the faint-hearted. Unless you are very accomplished at the shot you might well find that, under pressure in a tight match situation, you revert to playing the pot red into the middle pocket.

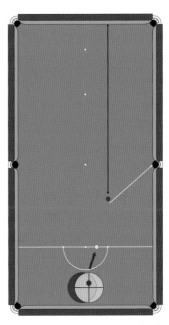

Start with the position shown, with the red in line with the end spot of the **D** and 22 inches (55.9 cm) from the baulk line, and the cue ball halfway between the end and middle spots of the **D**. As the red is a reasonable distance from the cue ball you can address quite close to centre ball and this will help you to impart as much momentum as possible into the cue ball, for a given cue speed. Aim for a three-quarter-ball contact, which is not as easy as the half-ball aim but is halfway between full-ball and a true half-ball.

You should find that the red travels directly up and down the table. If it goes to the right of this line you are hitting it too thick and, to the left of the line, too thin. You don't need to hit the shot quite as hard as for a standard middle-pocket loser, because the thick contact puts more pace into the red. Push through the line of the shot to achieve a long follow-through. Make sure that you miss the near jaw (sometimes called the near *knuckle*) of the middle pocket. Hitting the knuckle will almost certainly cause you to miss the shot.

Some experienced players employ the use of check side to help the cue ball run through the red, and you might find that this is something that helps you make the shot. Bear in mind though, that any application of sidespin complicates the shot, as the setting angle and the path of the red will be different from a shot played without sidespin.

Once you are comfortable with this in-off try similar red positions, setting the cue ball yourself. Do not be disappointed if you are unable to make these shots consistently from the outset as they are more challenging than they look. It might take you a long time to master the three-quarter-ball aim and, more importantly, to learn to judge the path of the cue ball after contact. However, it is definitely worth spending a good amount of time practising this shot as, in match-winning billiards, this one shot alone can be devastating and a sequence of in-offs into the middle pockets can become almost mesmerizing to watch.

You might find it quite a challenge to gain consistency with the pace of middle-pocket losers, so that you can bring the red back to a good position each time.

> **In case you were wondering…**
>
> For a given cue speed you will impart maximum momentum to the cue ball by using centre ball striking. The further you address away from the centre the less momentum will be imparted.

There are two things that might help with this. Firstly, try to use the same address on the cue ball for each shot. Secondly, try to make the same contact every time. Providing that you do these two things, your cue arm will have to repeat a similar action for each shot and you should get more consistency with the pace of the red.

Remember
✓ Address near to centre
✓ Push through the line of the shot
✓ Keep the red on a straight path

Try to avoid
✗ Altering the address and contact

The Drifting Cannon against the Nap

A cannon using throw and the effect of the nap, causing the cue ball to drift onto the second object ball

This is a clever shot that looks to be impossible, but can be made by taking advantage of the effect of the nap when playing down the table. Although the balls are nearly lined up it is still possible to play the run-through cannon.

Play the shot with *running side*, in this case right side. The side will throw the white to the left and, as the cue ball spins against the nap, it will drift towards the red.

Practise playing the shot by setting the balls approximately as shown, such that if you were to hit the white full-ball it would hit the red at a true half-ball. Play the run-through so that the white *just* misses the red and make sure that the cue ball *just* reaches the red. You will

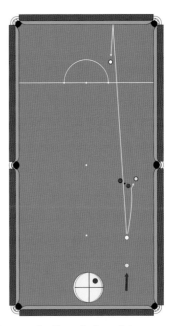

need to address above centre because the cue ball and the white are reasonably close together. When the balls are much further apart than this the shot becomes unreliable because it is exceedingly difficult to get an accurate white path in order for it to just miss the red.

Remember
✓ Make sure that the white just misses the red

Try to avoid
✗ Hitting the shot too hard

Lesson One

The Full-length Run-through
A forcing run-through loser played along the full length of the table into a corner pocket

As forcing run-throughs along the length of the table, these shots are quite a challenge. Nevertheless, they are lovely shots to practise and, as long as you apply plenty of sidespin, are easier than you might think.

With the nap, you will need cushion sidespin. Set the balls as shown and concentrate on a high address and smooth cueing. For these shots it is essential to push through the cue ball with a decent follow-through.

When playing *against* the nap, apply non-cushion sidespin and make

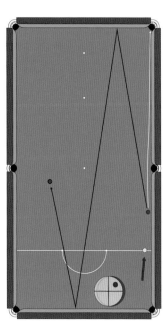

sure that the cue ball *just* reaches the baulk pocket.

If the cue ball is travelling too fast as it reaches the pocket, you will probably find that the sidespin keeps it out. When the cue ball is close to the object ball, as shown in this diagram, address very high on the cue ball.

Remember
✓ Use a high address
✓ Cue smoothly and make a long follow-through

Lesson One

The Long-range Run-through

A run-through loser spinning the cue ball along the side cushion into a top pocket

This drag run-through is an excellent practice shot and can help to improve your cueing. Although these shots are not terribly common in a game of billiards, mainly because they are fairly low percentage shots, they do crop up from time to time, particularly off the white after the break-off.

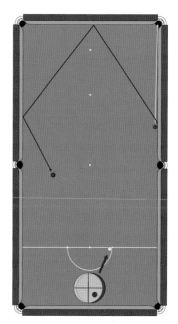

It is worth noting that this run-through can be played in an alternative way, by playing a forcing run-through at an exceptionally fast pace and addressing very high on the cue ball. However, playing a similar shot to a bounce-along run-through is not the best way of playing the shot.

Set the red somewhere near the position in the diagram and the cue ball near the right side of the **D**. Concentrate on pushing your cue through the cue ball, addressing at 4:30. Don't hit the shot too hard or the cue ball might still be skidding when it reaches the red. Play the run-through at a medium pace to bring the red to the middle pocket area.

Remember
✓ Address at 4:30
✓ Follow through smoothly

Try to avoid
✗ Hitting the shot too hard

Lesson One Summary

- *With* the nap, cushion sidespin causes the cue ball to drift towards the cushion, but *against* the nap cushion sidespin curves a ball away from the cushion. Slow-moving, fast-spinning balls deviate the most.

- Short jennies and long-range jennies are played with drag combined with sidespin. Long jennies are played by addressing above centre with sidespin.

- You need to adjust your aim when using sidespin because the cue ball pushes off line (*squirts*) as you hit it.

- The amount of swerve obtained is dependent on cue elevation.

- Drag prevents a roll-off and preserves sidespin on the cue ball.

- Sidespin helps a ball to run through.

- If you can manage it, the best way to play cushion run-throughs is by addressing below centre.

- When you are faced with challenging positions, consider the risks and rewards of the various shot options.

- If possible, select a shot that will keep both balls in prime position.

This lesson introduces the concepts of *stun* and *screw*, along with many shots that rely on these effects. You will also learn a couple of extremely useful guidelines that should make it easier to judge some of these shots.

There is also quite a lot of information about the effect of sidespin on shots employing one or more cushions.

Finally, you will find descriptions of many of the shots that use various combinations of sidespin, with stun or screw, to achieve a good positional outcome.

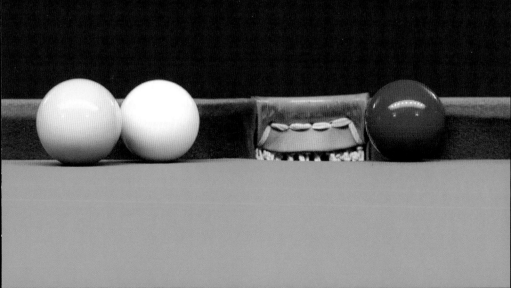

Concept: Ball motions

In order to play stun and screw shots it will help if you understand how a cue ball reacts to different addresses and cue delivery speeds.

Many of the shots in billiards are played using *natural roll*, which is a term used to describe a ball that is simply rolling, not skidding, with no backspin or sidespin. To get natural roll from the outset you need to address the cue ball as high as possible.

However, when you lower the address on the cue ball, say to centre ball, for a while it will not *rotate* at the same rate as it moves across the bed of the table, and is said to be *skidding*. It might even slide across the cloth with no forward or backward rotation whatsoever, although of course it might also have some sidespin applied. It will continue to skid before eventually beginning to roll. How long the cue ball skids is dependent on how low you address and how hard you hit the cue ball. For a given address, the harder you hit the shot the longer the cue ball will skid.

> **In case you were wondering…**
>
> Practically speaking, you can't make the cue ball spin forward faster than it rolls forward. The best you can do is to get it rolling naturally from the outset. If you address the cue ball as high as possible the lower edge of the tip will impact about halfway up from the centre of the ball.

A *stun shot* occurs whenever the cue ball, while skidding across the cloth with no backspin or forward roll, contacts an object ball. If this contact happens to be full-ball then the cue ball will stop dead in its tracks, and this specific case is known as a *stop shot*. Also, sometimes the cue ball will stop briefly before following through a small amount, and this is known as a *stun run-through*. For this to happen, the cue ball must still be skidding at impact but with a very small amount of forward rotation, so that it is just about to start rolling.

When you lower the address even further the cue ball will carry backspin, rotating backwards for a while as it moves forwards. How long the backspin lasts depends on how low you address and how hard you hit the cue ball. Friction will gradually reduce the backspin until there is none left and eventually the cue ball will start to roll, but in between rotating backwards and rolling forwards there is a brief period when the cue ball slides across the cloth. This skidding period only lasts for a *very* short time and you can't do anything to prolong this event, although you can adjust the point at which it takes place by altering the address or the pace of the shot.

A *screw-back* occurs whenever the cue ball is still carrying a good amount of backspin when it hits the object ball at a thick contact. On contact with the object ball the cue ball will hesitate for a short time, as it grips on the cloth, before spinning back. Of course, the more backspin it has the further the cue ball will come back. What might not be obvious is that, at full-ball contacts, if there is insufficient backspin to overcome the friction from the cloth, the cue ball will either stop dead or come backwards a very small amount.

This first diagram indicates the movement of the cue ball after being hit firmly, *just below centre*. You can see that the skidding period is quite extensive.

The next diagram indicates the movement of the cue ball after being hit *very low*. Initially it rotates backwards, whilst moving forwards. You can see that there is only a brief period of skidding that separates the transition from backspin to natural roll.

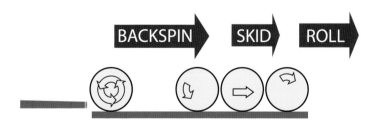

Concept: Stun

Having looked at various ball motions, it's now worth considering three distinct methods that you can employ in order to play a stun shot.

The simplest way is to play a firm shot with an address just below centre, so that the cue ball skids until it hits the object ball. The cue ball never starts to roll and, when the distance between the cue ball and object ball is small enough, even centre ball striking can result in a stun shot because the cue ball will not have time to begin rolling naturally before contact; there is no backspin present and the cue ball skids from the outset. This type of stun shot is especially useful for potting because you don't need to worry about the fast pace of the object ball.

A slightly more advanced way of playing a stun shot is by applying backspin, striking the cue ball well below centre. You have seen that, after the backspin wears off, the cue ball will momentarily skid before beginning to roll. If you judge the shot such that contact with the object ball is at that precise skidding moment, you will play a stun shot. This is more difficult to achieve than using the previous method unless you are making a full-ball contact. Practically speaking, stop shots are relatively simple to play when using a very low address as there is a decent margin for error and the cue ball can actually be rotating very slightly as it hits the object ball. A surprisingly easy way of playing a stop shot is to play at a strength such that the cue ball does not have the energy to spin back, even though it still has some backspin at the time of contact. Although the cue ball is rotating at the time of impact, the cloth friction is sufficient to stop any backwards motion across the bed of the table. With practice this is quite simple to achieve.

The most challenging stun shot is the stun run-through. This is more difficult to play than a basic stun shot because you need to judge the exact moment when the cue ball is just starting to roll. These shots are only useful for contacts near to full-ball and are usually played quite firmly, at a similar address to that required for a stun shot. One advantage of stun run-throughs is that the fast pace ensures that there is no roll-off. Stun run-throughs can be fairly easy to control at close range but at longer distances they become very challenging indeed.

Cue drill: Stun

This drill will help you to play stun shots at different distances. Initially, place the red on the spot and set the cue ball at the position nearest to the

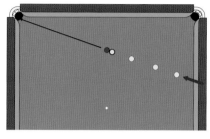

red. Play a stop shot, addressing *just* below centre, to pot the red. The cue ball should stop in a position so that you can just replace the red on the spot afterwards. Of course, these stop shots can only be made at full-ball contacts. When you are confident with this, play a similar shot from the other two cue ball positions. As the distance between the cue ball and the red increases, address fractionally lower and play at a slightly faster pace to make sure that the cue ball is still skidding when it reaches the red.

Now practise stop shots from these same three positions, but this time with a *very low* address. You should play these stop shots much more gently than the previous ones, but once again you will need a little more pace as the distance between the cue ball and the red increases.

During some of your attempts to stop the cue ball you will have noticed that, by mistake, it followed through a little. In other words, you inadvertently played a stun run-through shot. Set the cue ball at each of the three positions shown and practise stun run-throughs to follow through just a couple of inches. Experiment with the address whilst using a reasonably fast pace for the shot, but don't be surprised if you find these shots quite a challenge.

Finally, it is worth practising stun run-throughs off almost straight pots off the spot, similar to the position shown. These shots can be particularly useful for retaining close control of the cue ball at the spot end.

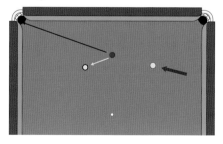

Concept: The 90° stun rule

If the cue ball is skidding on contact with an object ball, it will leave the object ball at approximately 90° from the path that the object ball takes. This is true for all object ball contacts, other than full-ball.

Cue drill: The 90° stun rule

Set the red on the pyramid spot and the cue ball for about a three-quarter-ball pot to the corner pocket. A stun pot will take the cue ball 90° from the red's path, towards the middle pocket. Try potting the red from different cue ball distances and angles, and a stun pot will always take the cue ball along the same line. At longer distances from the red you will find it easier to play a firm stun shot, addressing just below centre. At closer  range, experiment with more delicate shots using a lower address.

Practically speaking, this rule is most useful, and easiest to judge, with thick contacts at around three-quarter-ball or thicker. At these thick contacts it is easier to judge the object ball path and at contacts approaching full-ball it is remarkably easy to judge the angle that the cue ball will take, as it will be almost 90° from its initial path.

The 90° stun rule is used in other cue sports, to determine whether the cue ball will possibly enter a pocket after contact. In billiards, if the angle between the three balls is a little more than 90°, you should have a decent chance of making a cannon by using stun at a thick contact. Of course, this rule can also be useful for stun losers.

**The 90° stun rule is easiest to apply
when making a thick contact**

The 90° Stun Loser

A stun loser when the angle between paths of the cue ball and object ball, after impact, will be about a right angle

One of the most useful shots that employs the 90° stun rule is a stun loser into a middle pocket, often needed after a middle-pocket loser when the object ball is left short of ideal position.

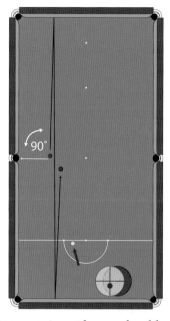

Set the red one ball-width past the centre of the table so that, with a stun in-off, it will take the path shown. To get pace into the red, play the shot at around a three-quarter-ball contact and the object ball should be directed up and down the table. Once you are confident with the shot, try applying some running side along with stun. This will keep the red well away from the left side cushions and is the best way to play

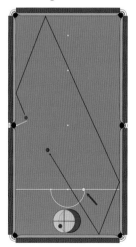

the shot. By using running side you should, after practice, be able to get the red to finish more centrally than in the diagram.

It is surprising how often this next stun in-off comes up during a game. The red should be taken in and out of baulk and can often end up in a similar position to where it started. You can apply some running side on these shots, depending on the exact angle. Sometimes if you need more than stun, use a small amount of screw. An advantage of understanding the

90° stun rule is that you can easily see if you have the angle for the stun shot, or need to adjust accordingly.

Be on the lookout for positions where you can adjust the contact to achieve a good positional outcome. Practise this shot, with the white near the corner pocket. Play a thinner contact than you would normally use for a stun shot, addressing lower and with some left sidespin, to control the path of the white. If you can get the white to follow the path shown you will have a large margin for error with the strength of the shot. Although the diagram shows the white being left for a drop cannon, had the shot been played too hard, a middle-pocket loser would have been available. By playing the shot this way you will always be able to recover the red, via a drop cannon, if it is out of position as shown. Note that if you were to play a thick contact and direct the white towards the centre spot area you could well be faced with a long loser, which is much less desirable than

a drop cannon. Play the shot from various other positions and find the limits from where you can make the shot and control the path of the white. This skill, of adjusting the contact and address to control the path of the object ball, is one of the most crucial aspects in break-building and you should always be on the lookout for the best positional outcome that you can manage.

The position shown here is similar to the last one and the 90° stun rule can be employed once again. However, this time the cue ball is a significant distance from the red, so it is best to play this in-off firmly, taking the red in and out of baulk. This is a more consistent way of stunning in-off, than attempting a delicate shot played with a very low address. Practise the shot by playing with a generous amount of running side because the side will help the cue ball to spin in off the pocket jaws. Make sure that you hit the shot hard enough, since the red will lose a good amount of momentum as it hits multiple cushions. Also, an over-hit shot should leave an opportunity of an in-off, whereas a shot played too softly could end in disaster, with the red in baulk.

This next shot is challenging and requires a lot of *feel*. It is best played slowly with running side and a small amount of screw. The running side helps to throw the cue ball wide, and causes it to drift via a small arc, into the pocket. You will probably find that, after practice, you will discover a favourite point to place the cue ball in order to play this shot.

Obviously, there are countless more positions from which you can play stun losers, using the 90° stun rule as a guide. If the shot that you are faced with is especially wide, you might have to change your choice of shot from a stun to a screw shot. For these more challenging shots, you might want to try  the technique of using *maximum screw* and adjusting your aim point until you think that the contact will be correct to make the shot. This method ensures that you only have to concentrate on one aspect of the shot—the contact.

Remember
✓ Usually play a firm stun shot at a thick contact
✓ Consider altering the contact (and address) for positional purposes
✓ Running side makes stun losers into corner pockets easier to make

Try to avoid
✗ Playing a delicate shot with a low address if you can get a satisfactory result by playing firmly with an address just below centre

The 90° Stun Cannon

A stun cannon when the angle between the three balls is about a right angle

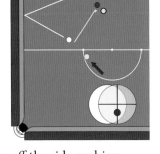

90° stun cannons are fairly easy to judge providing the cue ball is reasonably close to the object balls. Another significant benefit of these cannons is that you can predict the cue ball's final position. Providing the shot is not played too hard and the cue ball hits the *second* object ball at near to full-ball it will stop more or less where the object ball was, removing some of the positional uncertainty.

This stun cannon is reasonably straightforward, as you can set the cue ball in the **D**. Play a gentle stun cannon to contact the red full-ball, bringing the white off the side cushion.

Of course the angle will not always be perfect for the 90° stun rule to apply, especially if you are not in hand, so you will need to adjust these shots accordingly. If the shot is *wider* than 90° you will need to

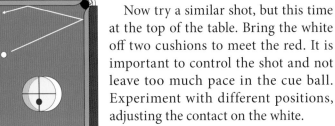

address lower on the cue ball.

Now try a similar shot, but this time at the top of the table. Bring the white off two cushions to meet the red. It is important to control the shot and not leave too much pace in the cue ball. Experiment with different positions, adjusting the contact on the white.

Stun cannons of a different kind can be used simply to score, with the end position being left partly to chance. Over longer distances you might not be able to control the positional aspect accurately and, in some cases, you will be content simply to make a cannon. The 90° stun rule should help you to judge some of these cannons.

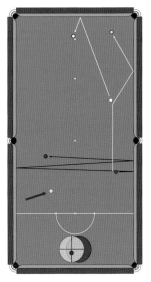

This is an awkward position, but you should have a reasonable chance of making a cannon. Set up the balls approximately as shown and see how successful you are at making this cannon. For longer distance cannons such as this, play a firm stun shot with a slightly below centre address. If you attempt this stun cannon by addressing very low, trying to judge the point at which the cue ball is skidding, you will find the shot *much* more difficult to make. You might be able to give some attention to adjusting the contact to bring the red to a better position than shown.

This is another challenging position where your main priority should be to score. Look carefully at the path that you would like the cue ball to take for a *direct* stun cannon, and you should be able to see that if you just miss the red on the left side, you might go in-off into the corner pocket. This increases the probability of scoring. Also, there is always the chance of making the cannon off one or more cushions, as shown.

Remember
- ✓ Look to hit the second object ball at near to full-ball
- ✓ For close-range cannons don't leave too much pace in the cue ball
- ✓ For long-distance cannons, give full attention to making a scoring shot

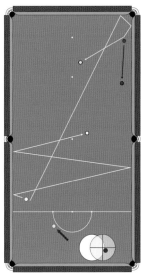

Lesson Two

Cue drill: Screw

Before moving on to play some screw cannons and in-offs, take the time to practise your cue action so that you can screw back comfortably.

Set the red on the pyramid spot and the cue ball about halfway between this and the billiard spot. Play a screw shot to bring the cue ball back to the top cushion, while the red comes off the baulk cushion to meet it. Properly played, the red should *just* reach the top cushion, although you might need to hit the red a little more firmly than this until you become accomplished at this drill.

To apply screw, hold the cue *lightly* and remember to pause at the backswing. The cue should be delivered crisply and you should feel the tip bite into the cue ball. Always remember to follow through smoothly. Also, avoid *quitting on the shot*, in other words deliberately decelerating the cue as you make the stroke. There is always a slight deceleration of the cue as the tip hits the cue ball, but all the same, push smoothly through the shot and the cue should be travelling at its fastest speed just as you hit the cue ball, and not beforehand. Make sure that your tip is very close to the cue ball as you address it, as this will help you to drive through the cue ball and limit the deceleration of your cue.

The timing required on these screw shots is more critical than on most other shots and it might take a considerable amount of practice before you can repeat this cue drill consistently.

The Screw Cannon
A screw-back to make a cannon and leave a good scoring position

Screw shots, particularly screw cannons, are extremely common during a game of billiards. Here, a screw shot is used to make a cannon, at the same time gathering the balls. Often, when playing these cannons, you will have to improvise in order to leave a good position afterwards, and the red is usually the critical ball to control. If you are screwing back onto the red, you will more often than not aim to leave a scoring shot off it. If the cannon is from red to white, then it will often pay to gather the balls or to bring the red into a scoring position.

Play the screw-back cannon shown to gather the balls for the next shot. Hold the cue lightly and feel the tip of the cue grip the cue ball during your delivery. Played correctly, the shot should finish with the balls in the corner pocket area.

> ### In case you were wondering...
>
> For shots played with a good amount of screw, the cue ball will spin back from the object ball at three times the angle that the object ball takes from the cue ball's initial path.

In order to give a greater margin for error with gathering cannons, a useful technique is to block the path of the first object ball with one or both of the other balls. This gives you a much greater degree of latitude with the pace of the shot.

This cannon is a common shot that is used to recover the red when it is in baulk. As you can never be absolutely certain of the contact that you will make onto the red, play the screw-back so that you don't hit the red too hard. Playing the shot this way will give you the best opportunity of leaving a scoring shot off the red. You can see that if the red had been hit slightly harder it would have ended up awkwardly placed near the baulk cushion, making it extremely difficult to continue the break.

This next screw cannon can be played to bring the red around the table to the top corner pocket area and to leave the white near the spot.

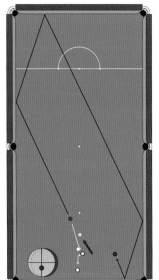

For this type of cannon, if the angle permits, it is usually best to bring the red off the side cushion before the top cushion as this slows it down and you will have more chance of leaving it in a good position.

Remember
✓ Hold the cue lightly
✓ Cue smoothly and get the tip to bite into the cue ball

Try to avoid
✗ Over-hitting the shot

Concept: Side on losing hazards

A spinning cue ball approaching an *open pocket* has a slightly better chance of entering the pocket than a ball without spin. The ball might bounce off one pocket jaw but will probably then spin in after hitting the other jaw. So in general, *any* side will usually help the ball into the pocket, although there's not much advantage to be gained if you are not playing near to a cushion.

However, a spinning cue ball running parallel (or nearly parallel) to the cushion, with cushion sidespin, has a *much* greater chance of entering the pocket than one without side. Conversely, a ball with the opposite sidespin has virtually no chance of entering the pocket.

**Cushion sidespin is absolutely essential
for in-offs along a cushion**

Cue drill: Side on losing hazards

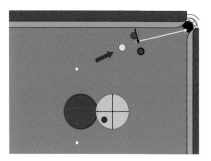

This thin loser, sometimes called a *skinny in-off*, is a shot that must be played with cushion sidespin. Without any side, this is an incredibly tough shot, but with maximum sidespin you would expect to get the shot most times.

Make sure that you get plenty of sidespin on by addressing at 7:30 and as near to the edge of the cue ball as possible. Hold the cue lightly and follow through smoothly. A light grip is particularly important for all thin shots such as this, as any tightness with the grip can cause a wider throw of the cue ball. If you play this shot correctly, the cue will do all of the work for you and you should find that you are hardly holding the cue at all after the shot has been played.

Concept: The 90° screw rule

If the cue ball impacts an object ball at a true half-ball with a significant amount of backspin, it will leave the object ball along a line that is approximately 90° from its original path.

Cue drill: The 90° screw rule

The most common shot that uses this rule is the 90° screw loser, played from a position similar to that in the diagram. These shots are played with screw, hitting the object ball at a true half-ball. The cue ball travels along the cushion to the pocket. If the angle is such that the shot needs to be played thinner or thicker than this, it becomes much more difficult because the 90° screw rule will not apply in those situations.

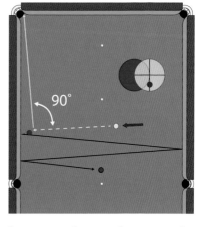

In case you were wondering…

On an average table the angle will not be 90° but will be closer to 84°, when coefficients of restitution and friction are taken into account.

Play the screw shot as shown in the diagram. You should be able to get the cue ball to follow a path towards the corner pocket, although for the moment you probably won't make the in-off because there will be no sidespin on the cue ball. In order to get the feel of this shot you will need to experiment with slightly different contacts that are close to the true half-ball.

Be aware though, that when close to the object ball, at distances of about 18 inches (46 cm) or less, it is possible to over-screw the shot, depending on your cue skills and the table conditions.

The 90° Screw Loser
A in-off played to spin the cue ball along the cushion into a corner pocket

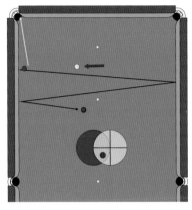

This shot is played using screw and maximum sidespin, striking the cue ball at 7:30. It is quite a difficult shot, requiring a certain amount of *feel*, so most of your concentration should be on making the shot, rather than the final position of the red. However, if you can judge the strength, leave the red away from the side cushions, as shown. On a standard shot the required contact is a true half-ball.

Initially place the red nearer the pocket than the diagram shows until you get used to the feel of the shot. Although you might be able to make the shot without any sidespin, this is only because the red is close to the pocket, so persevere with applying the sidespin. Once you are confident with the shot, move the red further from the pocket and also move the cue ball so that it remains level with the red, keeping the angle to the pocket the same.

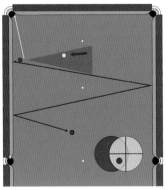

When you are confident with the standard shot, try adjusting the angle and playing the shot from anywhere within the shaded area. When above the red (nearer the top cushion), you will need a slightly thicker contact as too thin a contact will sometimes result in the cue ball hitting the cushion just after the red, causing a missed shot. Make sure that you apply sufficient

Lesson Two

screw for shots at these angles. Conversely, when below the red, play the shot thinner to avoid the double kiss. Also, a thick contact here would result in the cue ball pulling away from the cushion.

Just how low you need to address the cue ball depends on its distance from the red, the pace of the shot and the thickness of the contact that you use. There is no easy solution to mastering this shot; play it repeatedly from the same position, getting the feel of the tip biting into the cue ball, before moving on to another position. If you have difficulty with it, try playing with maximum side and screw, only adjusting the contact to make the shot.

Screw losers are slightly more difficult *across* the nap because the sidespin does not help the cue ball to grip the cushion. Also, screw losers will work *against* the nap, although they must be played at a faster pace than the standard shot. This is to stop the nap curving the cue ball away from the pocket.

The 90° screw loser becomes much easier when the object ball is near a corner pocket. As a general rule, it is best to use *running* side whenever the object ball is within about 9 inches (23 cm) of the pocket. The running side widens the throw of the cue ball after contact and this makes the shot easier to play, as you can often stun the shot, rather than use screw. Also, since the distance between the object ball and the pocket is small, you can be fairly sure about making the shot 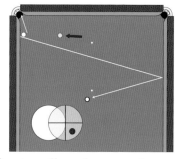 and confident that the non-pocket sidespin will not have an adverse effect. You can even play these shots without sidespin, if you prefer.

Remember
✓ For the standard 90° screw loser use maximum sidespin
✓ Shots at different angles require different contacts
✓ Play shots against the nap at a faster pace
✓ Use running side if the object ball is near to a pocket

Concept: Screw with reverse sidespin

If you screw back with right side
and the cue ball hits a cushion,
it will go to the left of you, and
vice versa. This can be useful in
positioning the cue ball for the
next shot. In the diagram, you can
see that the right sidespin takes the
cue ball to the left, after it hits the top cushion.

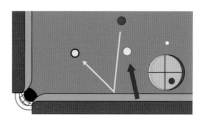

Using reverse sidespin is extremely useful when playing screw
in-offs where the cue ball will travel along, or nearly along a cushion.
For these shots you need to impart *non-cushion* sidespin, causing the
cue ball to spin off the jaw(s) and into the pocket. This is something
that will be made use of in the next shot, the reverse-side screw loser.

Cue drill: Screw with reverse sidespin

Set the balls as shown and practise a screw-
back onto the top cushion, using reverse
sidespin. Remember that a light grip will
help you to impart spin. Concentrate on
getting a decent amount of side on the cue
ball and don't worry too much about where
the red finishes. You should be able to play
this screw-back consistently before moving
on to the next shot.

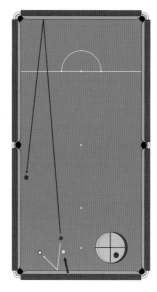

Lesson Two

The Reverse-side Screw Loser
A screw-back played with reverse side to spin along the cushion into a corner pocket

This is an extremely useful shot that is easier to make than it looks. On a table with a good nap the shot is not difficult, providing you are playing into a top pocket. The shot is played with a generous amount of side and screw, striking the cue ball at 7 o'clock. It is vital to control the pace of the cue ball, allowing the nap to work on it, so that it curves towards the side cushion as it travels towards the pocket. If the cue ball hits the pocket jaws, it should have sufficient sidespin to whip it into the pocket. Avoid playing the shot too fast because you won't get the benefit of the nap effect.

Set up the balls as shown in the diagram. Firstly, play the in-off without any side at all, to get the feel of the contact and pace of the shot. You probably won't make the in-off, but if you can get the cue ball to hit the pocket jaws it will be time to progress to attempting the shot using sidespin.

Now address at 7 o'clock and concentrate on applying a decent amount of sidespin, along with backspin. When you are comfortable with the shot, move the balls further from the pocket, keeping the same distance from the cue ball to the red.

Similar shots can be played across the table but these are a little more challenging because the nap will not curve the cue ball towards the cushion. Also, these shots can be played into a baulk pocket, but

Lesson Two

in these cases the nap will curve the cue ball *away* from the cushion, especially if they are played slowly. Nevertheless, still use reverse side

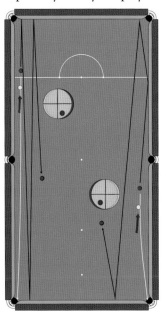

but make sure to play at a faster pace to limit the nap effect.

With good cue delivery and timing, the reverse-side screw loser can be made at any distance from a corner pocket. When practising, keep the distance from the cue ball to the object ball short, but the distance from the object ball to the pocket can be as long as you wish. Practise the shot with the object ball close to the middle pocket, as shown on the right side of this diagram.

Perhaps you have seen exhibition shots from positions similar to that shown on the left side of the diagram, to screw back all of the way along the side cushions, with reverse sidespin, into a top pocket. You might want to try these reverse-side screw losers with a long distance from the object ball to the pocket; they are easier than they look!

Finally, now that you have learned both the 90° screw loser and the reverse-side screw loser, take the time to learn shots that combine both of these techniques. Practise making these in-offs from anywhere within the shaded area shown in the diagram.

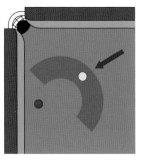

Remember

✓ Address low and apply a generous amount of sidespin
✓ For shots along the side cushion into a top pocket, play at a pace which will allow the nap to work on the spinning cue ball
✓ Play shots into a baulk pocket at a faster pace

Lesson Two

Concept: Controlling all three balls

When making a cannon, learning to control all three balls is one of the most valuable skills to master in order to improve your game. You will often have the opportunity to change the way you play a shot by adjusting any combination of address, pace and contact on the object ball. Often, this will make the cannon more of a challenge, and the best choice of shot might not be obvious at first sight.

When the cue ball is rolling naturally, shots narrower than the natural angle can be played in two distinct ways, thin or thick. For example, you might be left with a quarter-ball cannon, but because the quarter-ball contact gives about the same cue ball deflection as three-quarter-ball, you could choose to play the three-quarter-ball shot for positional purposes. A common error is for a player to see that the shot can be made at a thin contact, but missing the option of using a much thicker contact for a different positional result.

Sometimes you will have the opportunity to use stun or screw, in order to gain a better position. For example, you might have a simple half-ball cannon that you choose to complicate by playing at three-quarter-ball with a stun run-through. In addition, sidespin can markedly alter the final position of the balls.

When making a decision regarding the best contact and where to address the cue ball, you will also need to consider the pace of the shot in order to visualize the position of the balls afterwards.

> ### In case you were wondering...
>
> After making contact with an object ball, the path of a naturally rolling cue ball will deflect by $27.3°$ for a quarter-ball shot and by $27.6°$ for a three-quarter-ball shot.

**When playing cannons consider all possible outcomes
and adjust the shot for the best positional result**

Cue drill: Controlling all three balls

Faced with this slightly wide cannon from red to white, it might be tempting to play a half-ball shot with running side. This would probably leave the red far from the top cushion and in a poor position. Set up the shot and play it at a three-quarter-ball contact with stun. You should be able to take the red to the corner pocket area and push the white behind the spot. Therefore, contact and stun are used to leave a good scoring position.

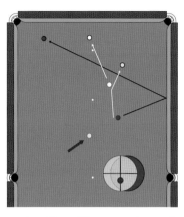

This shot could be played slowly, as a naturally rolling run-through cannon, but if you play it this way you will probably leave the red in

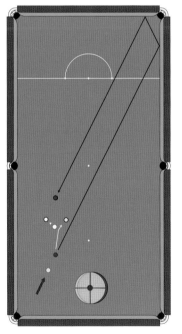

a poor position, perhaps near the side cushion. Also, it is usually a poor choice of shot to attempt to leave the red over a baulk corner pocket.

Play the shot as a stun run-through, bringing the red in and out of baulk, to gather the balls. Make sure that you hit the red with a thick contact, as errors in contact on the *thin side* will cause you to miss by quite a large margin.

So you can see that although a naturally rolling run-through would have been easier to play, by changing the shot to a more difficult stun run-through you can gather the balls.

This next position at the spot end can lead to trouble as the balls are slightly awkwardly placed, being too wide to make the indirect cannon with a half-ball shot played with running side. It is often poorly played as 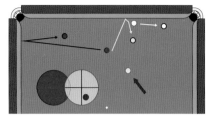 a five-shot, potting the red and stunning onto the white. The cannon is often seen as *insurance*, just in case the pot is missed. Also, the red will sometimes hit the jaws of the pocket and run along the side cushion out of position. More often than not, the cue ball will hit the white fairly full and end up close to the top cushion, with the white coming off the cushion into a poor scoring position.

Another frequent mistake is to take the red off the top cushion followed by the side cushion, leaving it some distance down the table. In this case, the only chance of a reasonable scoring opportunity would be if the white finished suitably placed for an in-off into the corner pocket.

The best way to play the shot is to make a *thin* contact on the red with *maximum screw*. Also, right sidespin will help to widen the cue ball's throw off the red and to make the cannon off the top cushion. Take the red off the side cushion to leave a reasonable scoring opportunity. So contact, screw and spin are used to improve the positional outcome.

Although there is a possibility of a gathering cannon here, there is also a simpler option to leave the balls in prime position. This cannon can be played with screw and some left sidespin, to knock the white out of baulk and into a position for a middle-pocket loser (from hand). As the red is contacted very finely, it will stay near the corner pocket. Played correctly, you will leave yourself a red loser and, after playing this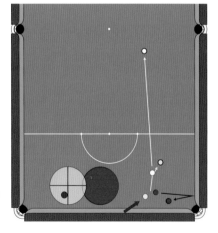

Lesson Two

in-off, you will be in prime position. It is essential to concentrate on leaving a red loser rather than a pot.

This last shot demonstrates how you can alter the final position of the balls, using contact and spin. This is a common position, with the red on the spot and the white awkwardly placed. If the white were nearer to the side cushion the long jenny would be on, but when it is positioned as shown in the diagram the long jenny becomes a tough shot and is usually not worth playing because it is so difficult to judge.

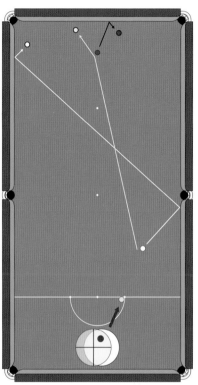

Contact the white as thick as possible, even up to three-quarter-ball and, in addition, make sure to get plenty of right sidespin on the cue ball. Both of these things help to bring the white to the top of the table. It is not possible to gather the balls, but you can bring the white to the corner pocket area. By doing this, you might give yourself another option, an in-off white, in case the cannon on the red does not push it into a decent scoring position.

If you play the shot without either the thick contact or the right sidespin you will not get the white to the corner pocket area, limiting your chances of continuing the break. The right sidespin transmits some left sidespin to the white, which helps it to run off the cushion to the left corner pocket area. Transmitted side is something that is covered later in this lesson.

Lesson Two

Concept: Cushion-imparted side

At moderate speeds, when a ball impacts a cushion at an angle (not square-on) it gathers a small amount of running side. Also, if it hits consecutive cushions (e.g. side/end/side) it will continue to gather running side. If it misses a cushion out, perhaps by hitting one side cushion followed by another, it will check off the second cushion.

**Each time a ball hits consecutive cushions it
gathers a small amount of *running* side**

Cue drill: Cushion-imparted side

Here, the red will run off the side cushion and continue to run as it hits the baulk and side cushions. This shot, known as a *cocked hat*, can be used as a shot-to-nothing, as it will probably leave the balls safe if the pot red is not made. (Although the in-off red is a far easier shot, you would probably end up double baulking yourself unless you played a fast, thin in-off, but this would make the shot much more difficult.) You might be surprised at how often you can make this cocked hat. Watch carefully and you will see the effect of running side as the red hits each cushion.

If you make the pot you will have a good chance to make the relatively easy in-off white. Alternatively, if you miss the cocked hat, you are very likely to leave the balls safe.

This next pot red at the spot end can be used to overcome a regulation that is occasionally applied in tournament play to force a cue ball crossing of the baulk line, from time to time. The cue ball is taken off five cushions, running off the first three and then checking off the

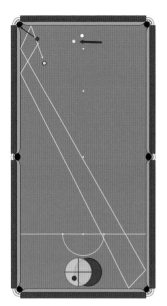

last two. As long as you control the cue ball path as shown, the last two cushions will slow down the cue ball and you can almost hit the shot as hard as you wish. Make sure that you do not miss the fourth cushion, because if you hit the top cushion beforehand the cue ball will continue to run and you will find it much more of a challenge to leave it in a good position.

Finally, this cushion-first cannon combines the applied left sidespin with some running side that is imparted by the cushion. Most players would attempt a cannon, hitting the white before the cushion, using right sidespin. This would cause the cue ball to *check* off the left side cushion, making the cannon extraordinarily difficult. You will need to hit the left side cushion reasonably close to the corner pocket if you want to make the cannon this way.

Play the cannon using a good amount of left side with a low address, hitting the *cushion first*. After contact with the white the cue ball should hit the left side cushion, somewhere near the point shown, before running onto the red. As long as the white is close to the side cushion, the margin for error is much greater with this shot than if you hit the white directly. You can hit anywhere close to the point

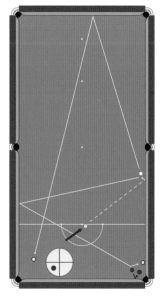

shown on the left cushion and still make the cannon. You might not be convinced about this and looking at a diagram may not be enough to persuade you. Try it out on the table and you will probably be amazed

Lesson Two

at the results. When practising it, make sure that the white is not too far off the side cushion because this makes the shot extremely difficult.

> **In case you were wondering…**
>
> Cushion-imparted side is different from the effect seen when a ball is driven hard onto a cushion. A fast *doubled* pot causes the object ball to rebound more sharply because the ball embeds itself into the cushion, distorting the rubber.

Concept: Screwing off a cushion

If backspin is present on the cue ball as it impacts a cushion, it will rebound at a sharper angle. This is very significant with maximum backspin and at fast speeds.

**Screwing off a cushion distorts the
rebound angle by sharpening it**

Cue drill: Screwing off a cushion

Play a slow, naturally rolling shot, at a medium speed, to see that the cue ball will more or less follow the dashed line. Now play the same shot with maximum screw and a fast pace to see the effect; the cue ball will follow a path something like the solid yellow line.

You might be wondering what use this concept has in a game of billiards. Well, it is extremely useful for cannons that seem to be impossible, particularly at the top of the table, when you are very close to the balls.

Lesson Two

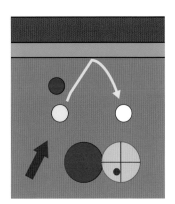

For the cannon shown, a thin shot with check side will slide around the back of the white, missing the cannon. Play the shot with *screw and check side*. You will probably be surprised at how easy it is to play, as long as you make a very thin contact.

It is important to apply the backspin without hitting this shot too hard. A flick of the wrist with a loose grip may help you to do this.

Concept: Transmitted side

When a spinning cue ball impacts an object ball, some of its angular momentum is always transferred, due to the friction between the two balls. The sidespin that is transmitted in this way is *very small*, so don't expect to see the object ball actually spinning. A better way to look at it is that the impacted ball will be made to *turn* a little, in the opposite direction from the spinning cue ball. The important point to remember is that this slight rotation can have a *significant* effect on the outcome of the shot, especially if the object ball is hit at a thick contact and then impacts a cushion square-on. If the object ball approaches a cushion at more acute angles, transmitted side has virtually no useful effect.

> **In case you were wondering…**
>
> At all contacts, other than full-ball, a tiny amount of spin is transmitted to the object ball even if the cue ball is not spinning at all. This effect is known as *collision-imparted* side and is similar in concept to *cushion-imparted* side.

**Transmitted side is *very* small but can
markedly affect position**

Lesson Two

Cue drill: Transmitted side

A good example of a billiards shot that uses transmitted side is this in-off with the object ball close to the top cushion. The result of the shot is markedly different when played with sidespin. One of the main reasons why this shot is so dependent on the side that is used is the fact that the white hits the cushion square-on.

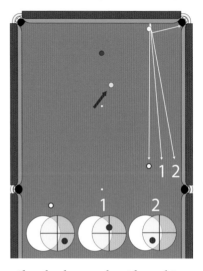

Play the in-off without any side and you will leave the white close to the side cushion, near to position 1. Now play it again, but using some check side. This time, the white will end up somewhere near position 2, perilously close to the side cushion.

Finally, move the white about ¼ inch (0.6 cm) closer to the cushion and play the shot with running side. A small amount of side will be transmitted to the white and because it is impacting the cushion square-on this effect is maximized and it will come slightly away from the side cushion, as shown in the diagram. You could improve this final position even further by contacting the white slightly thinner (and with more pace, to make the in-off). While the running side alone will leave a good positional outcome, combining this with a slightly thinner contact will always leave the white well away from the side cushion.

Transmitted side is most effective when the object ball hits the cushion square-on

The above shot is all that you need to prove to yourself that the use of transmitted side is essential in order to play advanced billiards, but in order to see exactly how much side is transferred, try the following drill.

Place the red on the middle spot of the **D** and the cue ball just behind an end spot. Stun the cue ball with maximum sidespin to get the red to hit *just outside* the baulk line and to come back into baulk. In the diagram shown, right sidespin

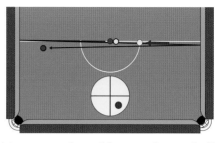

is needed to make this happen. To prevent the red hitting the cue ball you might have to use your cue to knock the cue ball out of the way as the red rebounds off the side cushion.

Although it is beneficial to employ transmitted side for a variety of in-offs, it also has many uses when playing cannons. The application of sidespin can make a huge difference to the end position of the balls. Play this next cannon from the position shown. Most players would play this shot with no side at all or, worse still, with running side, especially as without playing a stun shot you could just make the cannon with running side. Running side is

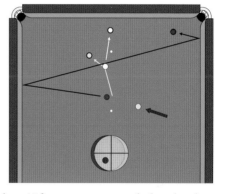

definitely the wrong side to use here! If you use stun and play the shot *without* any sidespin, you will separate the red and white and leave the red well away from the corner pocket. Running side makes matters even worse. However, play a similar shot with *stun* and *check side* off the red and the red will take on enough side to rebound at a much better angle off the cushion and come to the corner pocket area. If you combine this transmitted-side effect with hitting the red as thick as possible, you will get a lovely positional outcome.

Lesson Two

The Gathering Cannon

A cannon, often played with stun or screw, to gather the balls together using one or more cushions

The drop cannon is one type of gathering cannon, where the balls are initially *well-spaced* and the objective is to bring them *together* at the spot end. Gathering cannons of a different kind are used when the balls are initially close together, but it is necessary to separate them before bringing them back together. These cannons can be truly impressive, particularly if one of the object balls is taken off multiple cushions.

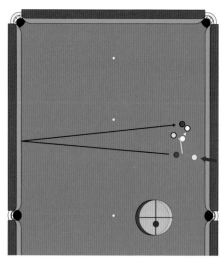

There are many kinds of gathering cannon, all with the same objective—to bring the three balls together. You will often need to improvise, as subtle adjustments in the address, contact and pace will determine whether the shot is a success. In particular, gathering cannons are commonly played with stun or screw and often make use of transmitted side.

This first cannon is a simple red to white stun cannon across the table. As the red will impact the side cushion square-on, any sidespin applied to the cue ball will markedly affect the path of the red as it comes off the side cushion.

Experiment with the position shown, playing the shot with extreme right and left sidespin; right sidespin will cause the red to come nearer to the middle pockets and left sidespin will cause it to go nearer to the top cushion. Stun the cue ball and hardly move the white.

For this cannon, the red will naturally follow a path off the side and baulk cushions to come back to the corner pocket area, close to the cue ball and the white. Make sure that the red is not too close to the cushion or it might *bed* into the cushion and give a different path to that shown. As you play the shot, you should be able to see the effect of the cushion-imparted sidespin on the red. For this cannon, concentrate on the path of the red and you will probably have to hit the shot harder than you may think. Something that is often overlooked in billiards is that cushions absorb quite a lot of a ball's pace, so this three-cushion shot needs *much* more power than if the

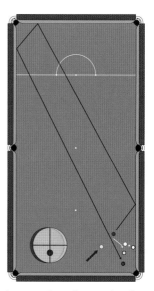

red were simply taken off a single baulk cushion. Also, for multiple-cushion paths, the distance travelled is greater, so friction has more time to slow the ball down.

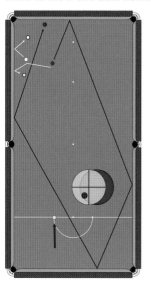

This position is a tricky one because there is a choice of shots. The cannon could be made from the right side of the **D** with a slight forcing shot (with no stun or screw) but this is a poor choice of shot because you will not gather the balls. It is far better to place the cue ball at the opposite side of the **D**, on the left side. Although this makes the shot more difficult, it gives an opportunity to gather the balls. Play the cannon very firmly and stun the cue ball from red to white. The red will follow a path similar to that shown, coming back to the corner pocket area. Some left sidespin will help to bring the red around the angles.

This last gathering cannon embraces several of the skills that you have learned. The white is just off the top cushion so if you play the screw cannon with reverse side, you will have more leeway with the shot. Of course it makes the cannon more complex if you use reverse sidespin, but once you are comfortable playing it this way you will have a greater success rate at the shot. If played without any sidespin, the white presents a small target and the cannon is likely to be missed.

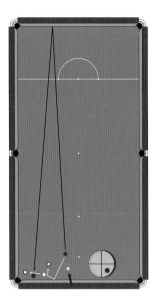

Another advantage of using reverse sidespin is that the red can be contacted slightly thicker. This, combined with the side that is transmitted, helps to direct the red towards the left side of the table. Practise taking the red off the baulk cushion to come back to the top cushion area, finishing near the corner pocket.

Remember
- ✓ Consider using any combination of stun, screw, sidespin and contact for position
- ✓ Reverse sidespin can be useful if an object ball is near a cushion
- ✓ Be sure to use enough pace when taking a ball off multiple cushions

Try to avoid
- ✗ Taking an easy option of just making the cannon without focussing on how to change the shot in order to gather the balls

Shot selection: Safety considerations

The two shots that follow highlight the importance of safety play and some of the principles that can be applied when faced with an uncertain scoring shot. Billiards is generally played in a flowing and attacking style and safety play is only a small part of the game. All the same, matches are occasionally won because of safety play or, more often, lost from the lack of it. Just as in other cue sports, it all comes down to the straightforward analysis of risk versus reward to make the best shot selection. It is worth emphasizing that if you feel that you are unlikely to make a scoring shot, you should consider your options for safety play.

In this position the white has been lost, with the red near the side cushion. Although you might feel confident about making the pot, what would your success rate be? Not only that, if you miss it, what would be the chance of leaving your opponent an easy opening? For example, let's say that you think you would make the pot 3 times out of 10 and you would leave an easy opening around 5 out of 10; these are poor odds and so perhaps in this case it would be better to consider a safety option.

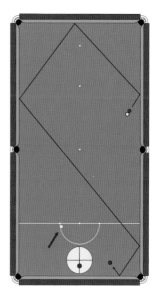

You could choose to stun the red around the table into baulk, leaving your cue ball near the side cushion, as shown. This is a fairly low risk shot that you could probably achieve more often than not, and your opponent might struggle to make a cannon from the resulting position. Of course, your opponent might reply with a safety shot, but either way, this stun shot would be a better percentage shot than the pot red.

A double baulk shot is another option. By playing a three-quarter-ball contact with some check side, the cue ball will follow a path to the top cushion and back to baulk and the red can be taken around the table and back to an area near the cue ball. If successful, this is a better safety shot than the previous one, but has more risk as it is relatively easy to get a double kiss on the red, leaving both balls in open play for your opponent. If you know about this shot, and have practised it, this might be the best option for you, but it will depend on your skill level and how you feel at the time.

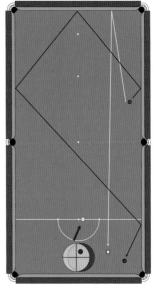

In all cases, you should make a sensible decision largely based on the probabilities of success and failure.

Consider the risks and rewards of the various shot options

There is often a lot to think about when faced with an uncertain scoring position that might require a safety shot. The following are just some of the points that might be worth considering, in the event that you miss the shot you are about to play.

When attempting a cannon, if *both* the red and white are safe, normally avoid disturbing the red as you might leave it near to a pocket for your opponent. However, if your opponent's ball is tight against a cushion this might influence your decision to leave it there and play off the red. If you do play off the white, make sure that a failed cannon attempt would not finish with your cue ball close to the red. You might consider playing a cannon as a shot-to-nothing, to leave the balls safe if you miss.

It is normally best not to leave balls so that they finish *slightly* away from a cushion, providing a big cannon target. You might have to adjust the pace of the shot, in order to do this. In the same way, an uncertain pot red (or an in-off) is often best played at a faster pace than normal, in order to avoid leaving the red or the cue ball close to a pocket, in case you miss the shot.

The Cross-table Loser
An in-off with the object ball near a pocket, allowing you to control its path significantly

With this in-off you should be able to control the path of the white to a large extent. The shaded area shows the approximate range of angles that you can make by adjusting contact and cue ball address.

It is usually wise to leave the white well away from the side cushions. For example, with the red on the spot it would normally be best *not* to attempt to position for a drop cannon, as it is remarkably easy to make a mistake and leave the white close to a side cushion.

Practise the shot using different contacts and amounts of sidespin to direct the white along various paths within the shaded area. Play a stun shot with a little right side, to take the white

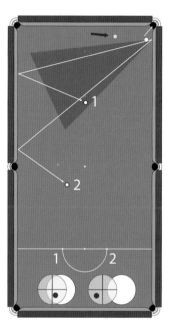

near to position 1. Once you are confident with this shot, play a thin contact with plenty of backspin along with left sidespin to cut the white towards the middle pocket area, near to position 2. With this shot, try to avoid doubling the white into the middle pocket and you will probably find that this is a much tougher shot than simply leaving the white around the pyramid spot.

Remember
✓ Use any combination of side, contact, stun and screw as required
✓ Keep the white away from the side cushions

Lesson Two

Shot selection: Minimizing risk

Here, you have the choice of a pot red, a cannon or a white 90° screw loser. The pot red is a risky shot, particularly because your cueing is likely to be hampered by the position of the white.

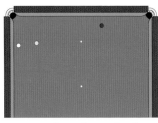

There is also a cannon from white to red using the side cushion, and possibly also the top cushion. The one-cushion cannon is trickier than it looks as it requires some check (left) side or a very thin contact. Cross-cannons such as these are never certain because when the first object ball is close to the cushion the outcome can be difficult to predict.

Notice that the red is sufficiently far away from the top cushion to enable the cue ball to slip around the back of it. These cannon positions depend so much on the red's proximity to the cushion. If the cue ball just can't get between the red and the cushion, the red becomes a much bigger target and the cannon is often worth a try. In this particular case the cannon might be slightly easier to play off two cushions rather than one as the white could be contacted slightly thicker.

However, most experienced billiard players would play the white loser and eventually look to manoeuvre the white for a drop cannon.

This next position also offers a choice of shots. A scoring shot off the red is definitely not the best option, as either the pot or in-off are much more difficult than playing off the white. Although the easiest scoring shot off the white is to play a firm stun loser, you would be likely to lose position by leaving the white close to a side cushion or possibly potting it into the left middle pocket.

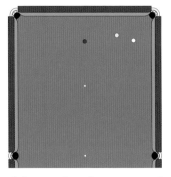

You could aim for a thicker contact to avoid the pot, but the positional aspect would still be uncertain.

The best way to play the in-off is to take the white as thin as possible, with maximum screw and some left side in order to leave a drop cannon. By keeping the white on the *right* side of the table you will find that you have a good degree of latitude with the pace of this shot, while still leaving the drop cannon. Even if you over-hit the shot by a large amount, you will probably leave a middle-pocket loser. Keeping the white on a path that gives a large margin for error with position is a much more effective way of gaining position than by stunning the white across the table.

In this last diagram, the red is out of position and the white is in baulk. The cross-table loser off the white can be played in one of several ways, depending upon the final position required.

Many players would attempt to position the white close to the red, but this is not the best choice of shot. For example, if the white lands in the smaller shaded area you will be left with a tricky screw cannon from the **D**.

It is best to play the in-off white to leave it anywhere within the larger shaded area, leaving you a choice of a white loser to the middle pocket or a white to red cannon.

To give yourself the best chance of continuing your break, when making your shot selection the best option will often be the one that has the least chance of going wrong. As a general rule, don't play *one* risky shot in an attempt to gain prime position when there is an opportunity of playing a *sequence* of shots that carry no risk.

Lesson Two

Lesson Two Summary

- The 90° stun rule is useful for stun cannons and can also be used for some in-offs.

- For screw shots it is crucial to have good timing and to hold the cue lightly.

- The 90° screw rule is useful for playing a screw loser along a cushion, using cushion sidespin.

- Cushion (pocket) sidespin is essential for in-offs along a cushion.

- When a ball hits a cushion (not square-on) it will gather a small amount of running side.

- Amazingly, screwing off a cushion will significantly change the rebound angle of the cue ball.

- Transmitted side is remarkably small but has a significant effect on some shots, particularly if the object ball hits a cushion square-on.

- Sometimes it might be appropriate to consider a safety shot, rather than try a more risky option.

- Avoid playing *one* risky shot in an attempt to gain prime position if there is an opportunity of playing a *sequence* of shots that carry no risk.

Lesson Three

Recovery shots

In this lesson you will learn about shots that can be played to overcome positional difficulties while making a break.

You will initially learn how to play some awkward losing hazards, where positional play is quite a challenge. The lesson then concentrates on many different types of cannon, particularly those using multiple cushions.

You will then learn all about single and double baulks along with various methods to recover balls in baulk. The lesson finishes with some advanced cushion-first shots.

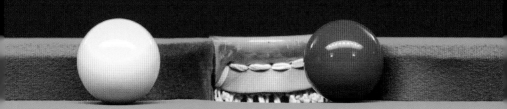

The Slow Long Loser

An in-off with the object ball near the centre spot, taking it off two cushions

When the red is to the side of the spots and just above the centre spot, the in-off is reasonably easy to make but the positional aspect is quite awkward. The best way to play this shot is to take the red off two cushions to leave it around the pyramid spot. Although the red *can* be taken off three cushions by hitting it slightly thinner than a true half-ball and playing at a fast pace, this is a low percentage shot and should be avoided as it is too easy to miss the in-off or to end up potting the red into a middle pocket.

Practise the shot from red positions within the shaded area. Play the shot slowly and contact the red at a thick half-ball. Concentrate on pushing through the line of the shot to get an accurate contact on the red. You might also find it useful to shorten your backswing to control the pace. You can use a hint of check side, although you might find it simpler to play without any sidespin.

Remember

✓ Play a thick half-ball at a slow pace
✓ Use a short backswing and push through the line of the shot

Try to avoid

✗ Deliberately taking the red off three cushions

Concept: The nap effect on naturally rolling balls

With the nap
When playing naturally rolling shots at *any* angle, balls do not drift enough to make any difference to the shot, even on tables with the heaviest of cloths. For example, the slow long loser that you have just played needed no adjustment for the nap. Similarly a slow pot off the pyramid spot into a top corner pocket will need no allowance for the nap because the object ball will travel in more or less a straight line.

Directly across the nap
There is very little practical effect, although a slow pot along the top cushion is easier than one along the baulk cushion because the nap fibres push the ball slightly towards the top cushion.

**Ignore the nap effect when playing shots at *any*
angle *with* the nap or *directly across* the nap**

Against the nap
The cloth fibres can be thought of as little needles, all pointing towards the top end of the table. When a ball moves with the nap it is moving away from the points of the fibres and there is virtually no effect on its path. However, when a ball is travelling against the nap the fibres are pointing towards the ball, resulting in a slight effect on its direction of travel. For example, a slow pot off the pyramid spot into a middle pocket can be aimed slightly towards the far jaw, allowing the nap to turn it in to the centre of the pocket. For medium or fast paced shots, the nap does not have time to curve the ball. Also, the direction of travel has a bearing on the curve of the ball and the two

Allow
for the
nap with
slow pots from
the shaded area

Don't allow for
the nap with these
slow pots

Lesson Three

slow pots shown, into the baulk pocket, would need no allowance for the nap. As a rough guide, a naturally rolling ball needs to be travelling on a path which is between about 30° and 60° against the nap for any significant drift to take place.

Make a small allowance for slow shots played diagonally against the nap

Cue drill: The nap effect on naturally rolling balls

This thin in-off, allowing for the nap, can sometimes get you out of trouble. There is also the added safety aspect, because if you miss the shot you can leave the red on the side cushion and you are unlikely to leave a scoring position for your opponent. Play the shot with enough pace so that you don't leave your cue ball in the jaws of the pocket should you miss the shot, but don't play it *too* hard.

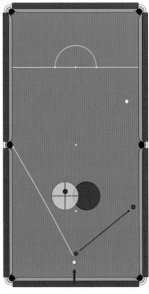

Also, try a slow pot red off the billiard spot into a middle pocket. You should be able

In case you were wondering…

It is becoming increasingly common to see shaved cloths, which curve the balls much less than a standard cloth. Professional snooker tournaments are played on these extremely fine cloths, with a nap that hardly causes a ball to drift at all.

to see how much the red curves on its way to the pocket. If you look carefully you will see the red drifting more as it approaches the pocket because it will be travelling slowly at this point.

Lesson Three

The Forcing Loser

An in-off played at a fast pace causing the cue ball to arc into the pocket

Forcing losers from hand can be some of the trickiest positional shots that you will be faced with. It is relatively easy to score from most of these shot positions but, if played without due care and attention, the chances are that you will not leave yourself an easy scoring shot afterwards.

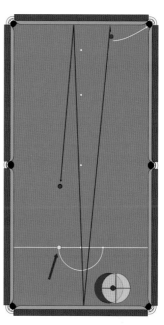

For long-range shots, centre ball striking gives the best chance of making the in-off as it helps to get power into the cue ball, although many of these shots will need to be played with some sidespin for positional purposes, as shown in the diagram. Also, on responsive cloths you will need to make sure that you don't stun the cue ball, so you might have to address slightly above centre.

A fundamental point about long-range forcing shots is that it doesn't really matter how much cue power you have and therefore how much you can force the shot. What *does* matter is that you know the limits from where you can play these shots.

In case you were wondering…

You'll get less power in the shot the further away from the centre that you address the cue ball, assuming the same cue speed.

Usually, the main challenge is to keep the red as far away from the cushions as possible. It is always worth looking to see if you can take the red off the side cushion at the baulk end of the table but, with the red on the right side of the table, this doesn't look possible. You might end

Lesson Three

up with the red finishing near the left side cushions or, even worse, ending up in baulk after hitting the jaws of the left baulk pocket. Play the shot with as thick a contact as possible in order to keep the red away from the left side cushions. The application of some check side will help to keep the red away from the cushions, but you might have more success if you play the shot without sidespin, especially if you find that you are having difficulty making an accurate contact at such a fast pace. The thick contact is the most crucial aspect of the shot.

Changes in object ball position will affect your decision on how to play the forcer. Set the red in line with the spots and about 15 inches (38 cm) from the billiard spot, with the cue ball on the end spot of the **D**. From this position you should not hit the red too thick and also, if you apply some running side it will help the red to miss the baulk corner pocket. Just as with the previous shot, if you prefer, you can play without sidespin because applying side is far less important than getting a good contact on the red. You will need to concentrate on the speed of the shot and it will be worth repeating the shot several times to get the feel of the pace required. The result will depend on your *touch* and *feel* as you push the cue through at this fast pace. The speed of the table will have a huge influence on the final position of the red and on fast tables you might have difficulty keeping the red away from either the top or side cushion as it comes to rest.

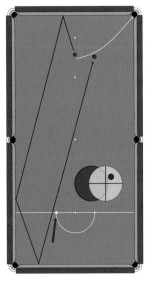

Once you are comfortable with this initial shot, move the red about one inch (2.5 cm) nearer the top cushion, and play the shot again. Repeat this practice sequence, incrementally moving the red nearer to the cushion, until it is about 11 inches (28 cm) from the spot. Of course, you will need more power in the shot as the red gets nearer to the top cushion.

This next forcer is from a position that is too wide for an in-off with running side, and the red is taken off the side cushion before the top cushion. Set the red equidistant from the centre and pyramid spots and 23 inches (58.4 cm) from the side cushion, with the cue ball on the end spot of the **D**. You won't get the same red-ball path every time, as with these power shots you will almost certainly be slightly inaccurate with the contact. You will probably find it easier to address fairly close to the centre of the cue ball although you can use a small amount of sidespin, as shown in the diagram, to help throw the red towards the side cushion.

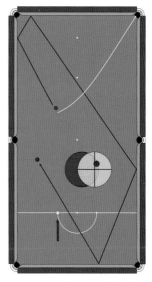

There are many other positions from where you can play forcing losers from hand, but to achieve a decent positional result you might have to *widen* the angle slightly so that you need to use more pace for the shot in order to get the object ball to travel in and out of baulk. Also, the location of the second object ball could influence your choice of shot, as you might be able to leave a position for a cannon.

It is impossible to describe how to approach every one of these shots because a small positional change might totally change the best way to play the shot. However, on most occasions you should use a pace and address that will give you the best chance of leaving the red away from the side cushions. A good practice routine is to set up a position for a forcing loser with the other object ball awkwardly placed; the objective being to make the in-off and eventually recover the other ball.

One thing that might not be obvious to you is that forcing losers can be remarkably easy when the object ball is near a cushion. Played correctly, the cue ball will initially throw wide and then travel in an arc that swings it into the pocket. For this reason these shots are sometimes referred to as *swingers*.

Lesson Three

Consider this seemingly awkward position, with the white in baulk. The in-off can be made quite easily by forcing the shot, as shown. To practise the shot, set the white behind the left spot of the **D** and two ball-widths away from the baulk cushion. Set the cue ball on a line joining the middle spot of the **D** and the white. Play the in-off with a high address and at a fast pace, allowing your cue to push right through the shot. As long as you address well above centre, shot success will depend on getting the correct pace. Once you become accomplished at it, move the white a little nearer the baulk cushion. In fact, the shot can be made quite easily from the same cue

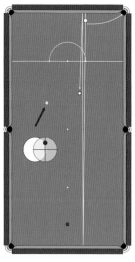

ball position when the white is only one ball-width off the cushion. You will need more pace as the white gets closer to the cushion.

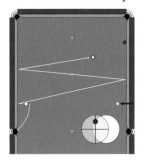

This last forcing loser is another relatively simple shot which might look quite a challenge if you are not used to playing it. Set the white about 12 inches (30 cm) from an imaginary line across the centre of the table and about two ball-widths off the side cushion. Place the cue ball level with the white on the opposite side of the table. Again, play the in-off with a high address and a fast pace.

Remember
✓ Concentrate on making an accurate contact
✓ For long-range shots, address near to centre ball
✓ For close to medium-range shots, use a high address
✓ Consider using sidespin for positional purposes

Try to avoid
✗ Leaving the object ball near a side cushion

Concept: Using running side for cushion cannons

For cushion cannons, side should normally be used to *run* off the cushions because check side makes the cue ball path unreliable. In fact, it is important to avoid using *any* check side when attempting cushion cannons, unless you are very close to both the cushion and the balls so that the shot is remarkably easy in the first place.

The use of running side on certain cushion cannons allows you to be slightly inaccurate with both side application and contact, but the shot must be at the correct angle in the first place. When playing from hand, take great care to set the cue ball accurately for the correct angle. These cannons only become unreliable at extremely thick contacts, because the cue ball will run through too much.

There is a certain degree of latitude with both contact and sidespin for cushion cannons played with running side

Cue drill: Using running side for cushion cannons

Set the balls as shown in the diagram, with the red on the spot and the cue ball set for a straight pot, at about halfway to the side cushion. Place the white not quite level with the red, about one ball-width further away from the top cushion.

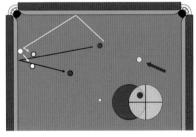

Aim for a true half-ball and use running side (off the cushion) to make the cannon. You should be able to make this cannon every time. Due to the running side, the contact on the red is not critical. Nevertheless, the position needs to be *on*, so it is crucial that the balls are correctly positioned for the shot.

Now hit the red too *thin*, up to about a quarter-ball. You will find that the cue ball will travel more quickly and at a more acute angle to the cushion, so the running side has less effect, meaning that you will still make the cannon. You can also hit the shot slightly thicker than the true half-ball and still make the shot.

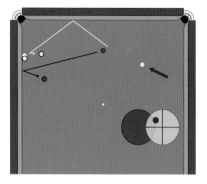

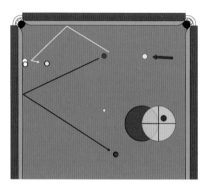

Compare this with the application of side to check off the cushion. This time set the cue ball *level* with the red and play a true half-ball shot with right side in order to check off the cushion. Providing that you make an accurate contact, you should find that this is the correct angle to make the cannon.

Now try making a deliberate mistake with the contact, playing thinner than normal, and you will find that you will miss the cannon by quite a large margin. Therefore, check side is best avoided when playing cushion cannons such as these.

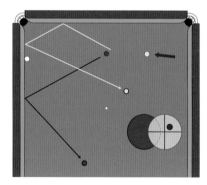

This next shot is a cannon that highlights how difficult it can be to play off cushions using check side. Begin by setting the cue ball about 7 inches (18 cm) from the end spot of the **D** and the white about 13 inches (33 cm) from the centre pocket. Use left sidespin, playing a true half-ball off the left side of the red. The cue ball will take a path off two cushions and make the cannon on most occasions. You might need to adjust the cue ball position slightly, within the shaded area, depending on table conditions.

Now play the shot again, but this time off the right side of the red. The left sidespin will check the cue ball as it impacts the cushion, and if you play *very accurately* you will make the cannon. However, you will find that you have little success with this one-cushion cannon because even the smallest error in contact and/or sidespin application will cause you to miss the shot. You will also find that the check side slows down the cue ball significantly, so that you will barely reach the white. Play a few of each of these running and check side cannons to convince yourself that check side yields exceptionally poor results.

Therefore, running off cushions usually gives a *much* better success rate than using check side. Unless you are very close to the balls, and with a short distance from the cushion to the second object ball, avoid check side when playing indirect cannons.

Normally avoid check side when playing cushion cannons

You might want to practise other set-position running side cannons off the spotted red. For example, with the cue ball on an end spot of the **D** and the red on the spot, a running side cannon will hit the side cushion about halfway from the baulk line to the middle pocket and hit the baulk cushion below the point from where the cue ball started.

The One-cushion Running Cannon

A cannon played with sidespin to run off a cushion and gather the balls at the spot end

This looks to be a tough cannon, but once you have set the cue ball correctly in the **D** you should get the shot every time. The setting of the cue ball is the key to this shot but once set, the white ball contact and amount of sidespin is not that critical.

Place the balls approximately as shown, with all three balls in a straight line to the corner pocket. Aim for a true half-ball with a good amount of running side (off the cushion), but slightly less than maximum. You should attempt to make the cannon and gather the balls near the spot end. Avoid playing the shot with too much pace and experiment with various amounts of side and different contacts. Once you are confident with this cannon, try some other shots from similar positions.

You might find it useful to look at the position of the balls from a different perspective, perhaps from the side cushion, to help you judge the setting of the cue ball in the **D**.

Remember

✓ Take time to set the cue ball accurately
✓ Use running side with a true half-ball contact

Try to avoid

✗ Hitting the shot too hard

Lesson Three

Concept: Using multiple cushions

It is a remarkable fact that when playing a long-distance cannon it is often *much* easier to get the cue ball to follow a desired path when using two or more cushions, rather than just one. A one-cushion shot can sometimes be the most difficult of all, particularly if there is any significant distance involved. One reason for this is that any unwanted sidespin on the cue ball can have a large effect on the angle that the cue ball will take off the cushion. You will probably find this difficult to believe, so consider the following position, with the white about 10 inches (25 cm) from an imaginary line across the centre of the table and about 9 inches (23 cm) from the side cushion. With this cannon, if you set the cue ball on the end spot of the **D** and contact the white at a true half-ball, with no sidespin, you should hit the red every time. This is assuming that your cueing is true and you do not impart any side. Therein lies the problem: true cueing is extremely difficult to achieve.

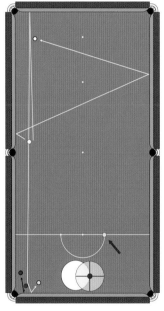

Any error in contact will mean that the cue ball will hit the top cushion at the wrong point. This error is then doubled as the cue ball rebounds off the top cushion; if the cue ball is just 1 cm *out* when it hits the top cushion it will be about 2 cm from the ideal path as it comes back past the white's original position, *and still travelling in the wrong direction.* As the cue ball still has more than half of the table to travel, the error is further amplified so that by the time it reaches the baulk cushion it will have missed the red by a significant margin. All of this is because of a small error in contact, but now consider the further problem of the effect of sidespin.

Lesson Three

One of the hardest things to do is to strike a cue ball without applying any sidespin whatsoever, and even top players find this difficult. Assuming you make the correct contact on the white, if you apply the slightest amount of right sidespin the cue ball will throw slightly right, hitting the top cushion to the right of the intended point. At this point the right sidespin amplifies the error and on impacting the cushion it will come further to the right side of the table. Left sidespin causes the opposite effect; the cue ball initially throws narrower, to the left, and then goes further left on rebounding from the cushion. Remember that in this case the detrimental effect of sidespin is more or less maximized because the cue ball is hitting the cushion square-on.

So although this cannon looks relatively easy, it is a tough shot and even a slight error in contact and/or application of sidespin will almost certainly cause you to miss the shot.

Cue drill: Using multiple cushions

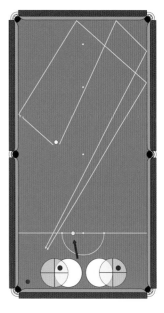

Set the white about 22 inches (56 cm) from the side cushion and about 10 inches (25 cm) from an imaginary line across the centre of the table, with the cue ball between the left and middle spots of the **D**. Play a true half-ball off the right side of the white with plenty of running side and you will find that the cue ball will always get close to the cannon. You will probably be amazed that even with errors in contact, or perhaps in application of sidespin, you will still get close to the red.

You might find it incredible that you can also make the cannon off the left side of the white, again using right sidespin to run off the cushions. This method is not usually employed, mainly because there is a risk of the cue ball kissing the white as it travels around the table, but it can be quite effective. In any case, you should get close to the cannon whichever approach you decide to take.

Now place the cue ball with an edge over the end spot of the **D** and, with the butt of the cue over the centre of the baulk pocket leather, play with a generous amount of running side. You might have to adjust your aim slightly, depending on the table conditions but, once you have found the aim point by looking backwards at the path of your cue over the baulk corner pocket, you should get very close to making this shot time after time. The fantastic thing about this shot is that if you put a little too much or too little running side on the cue ball, you will still make the cannon. If you are not convinced, try playing this shot *without taking much*  *care* and you will see that the cue ball will return to baulk at almost the same position every time. You can be inaccurate with your cueing and yet still make the shot!

It is interesting to compare this three-cushion shot with a shot played directly off the top cushion. Place the cue ball with the left edge midway between the middle and right spots of the **D** and aim over the centre spot. You will find a path towards the left

In case you were wondering...

Most cannons where the cue ball has a long way to travel after contacting the first object ball are best played slightly thinner than the thick half-ball, at the true half-ball contact, because this gives more momentum to the cue ball.

baulk corner pocket if you cue accurately, but without taking much care you will see that the cue ball will return to baulk at quite different positions. Also, the harder you hit the cue ball the more any unwanted sidespin affects the shot because it doesn't wear off by the time the cue ball reaches the top cushion.

So, in summary, although it is usually easier for the eye to judge an angle off one cushion, playing the shot using two or three cushions will often give a much better success rate.

Finally, here is the *spotted balls* position. There is a two-cushion cannon that is reasonably easy to make, although generally not one that should be played in preference to the long loser.

Set the cue ball for a standard long loser into the *right* corner pocket but, instead of playing the in-off, attempt the cannon. By playing a thick half-ball contact on the *left* side of the white and running off two cushions, the cannon is much easier to make than it looks. You will find that you can achieve a high success rate at cannons using multiple cushions, even over these long distances.

For some indirect cannons it is best to use running side off multiple cushions

Concept: Target size

Before attempting an all-round cannon it is important to assess whether there is a reasonable chance of hitting the second object ball. Normally, the target ball needs to be in the vicinity of a cushion to make these cushion cannons worth trying. The biggest targets are found when the cue ball can *almost* get around the back of the object ball.

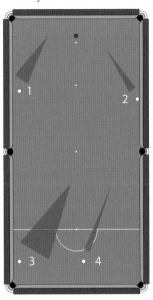

With the cue ball in hand, in order to hit the red and make a cannon at position 1, the white is an ideal distance off the cushion. The cannon will be made if the cue ball follows a path anywhere inside the shaded area. It is worth being on the lookout for object balls that are nicely positioned near to a cushion.

For position 2, the white is tight on the side cushion so the cushion does not increase the size of the target by much. It is true that the cue ball can make the cannon if it hits the cushion *just* before the white, but there's not much margin for error here. Nevertheless, this white position is slightly better than one with the white well away from the cushion.

For position 3, the white is close to the side cushion and in baulk. The target size is very large, and you should get a scoring shot if the cue ball follows any track within the shaded area. Even if you miss the cannon you might find the baulk pocket instead.

For position 4, the shaded area is tiny because the white is well away from any cushion and it is incredibly easy to go around the back of it. There is, of course, a small chance that you could make the cannon off the baulk cushion!

**Consider the cue ball path and object ball target size
when playing long-distance cannons**

Set-position Cannons

Shots played from hand off the spotted red in order to make a cannon with an awkwardly placed white

These cannons are worth memorizing as they occasionally crop up as set-positional shots during a game. There are many other set-position cannons that can be practised, and you might wish to experiment with cue ball positions outside of the **D** as well as different white locations.

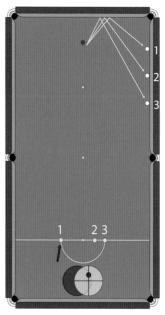

The diagram shows where the cue ball should be positioned for the various cannons. As the cue ball does not have far to travel after contacting the red, play these shots at a thick half-ball, but avoid hitting the red *too* thick. It is also important not to impart any check side, so make sure that you cue accurately in order to do this. Play at a medium pace; it is a common fault to play these shots with far too much pace. You should attempt to leave the red near the left middle pocket for the next scoring shot. Practise the three cannons shown until you are comfortable with them, trying each time to bring the red to the left middle pocket area. Finish off by placing the white between positions 1 and 2 and work out where to place the cue ball in the **D**.

You can see that with all of these shots you are separating the balls and, although the cannons are easy to make, it is quite a challenge to leave a scoring position for the next shot.

There is another way to play the cannon with the white at position 1, and this is by playing a very firm shot and taking the red in and out of baulk and back to the vicinity of the white. To do this, place the cue ball about one quarter of the way from the middle spot to the end spot of the **D**. Play firmly to bring the red around the table to the corner pocket area. Providing you make a good contact on the red, shot success will depend on getting the correct pace.

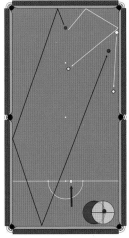

Sometimes you might wish to play a cannon to leave the red near to a baulk pocket, although

this is normally not the best shot option and not one that is usually employed by top players. From this position, you can play the cannon to double the red to the left baulk pocket area, but there is not much margin for error with position because the red will travel quite close to the left side cushions.

Practise playing the cannon with the white on the side cushion and about halfway between the spot and the pyramid spot, with the cue ball on the middle spot of the **D**. You will need to make sure that the red misses the middle pocket jaws. Played correctly, you will leave the red near the baulk pocket for an in-off.

Remember

✓ Aim for a thick half-ball
✓ Memorize these positions

Try to avoid

✗ Hitting the red too thick

Concept: The 90° initial separation rule

> *When the cue ball hits an object ball the two balls initially move apart at approximately 90° to each other.*

Of course, this concept does not apply to full-ball contacts. Also, the wide deflection is not for very long, because the cue ball soon arcs back on line. For example, with a thick half-ball contact, the object ball is directed at an angle of about 28° from the initial cue ball path. The cue ball will initially be deflected about 62° (90° – 28°)

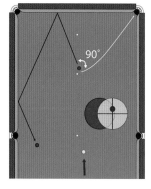

from its initial path but, after a brief moment, will arc back to the standard thick half-ball deflection angle of about 34°.

In case you were wondering...

A consequence of the 90° initial separation of the balls is the 90° stun rule, as the cue ball never comes back on line, due to the stun.

So, for a *short* time the cue ball throws *exceptionally wide*, before coming back on line (assuming it is not played with stun). For most shots this isn't noticeable, but when there is a ball or a cushion close to the object ball it becomes exceedingly important.

Cue drill: The 90° Initial separation rule

Set this cross-loser off the red with the white 4 inches (10.2 cm) from the spot. There appears to be plenty of room for the cue ball to make the in-off red, but play the shot to find that it hits the white about half-ball! The white gets in the way before the cue ball has time to arc back to the half-ball line for the in-off, and this is the case for even very slow shots.

Now try this shot, with the red on the centre spot and the white placed so that the edges are aligned both along and across the table. Play the long loser off the red, which looks impossible, and the initial cue ball deflection will take it around the white before it arcs back towards the corner pocket.

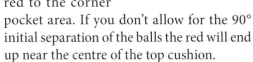

This next cannon is one that is often badly played because not enough allowance is made for the initial cue ball deflection. Set the balls as shown and try to make the cannon to push the red to the corner pocket area. If you don't allow for the 90° initial separation of the balls the red will end up near the centre of the top cushion.

Finally, play this cannon at the top end. Remember that the cue ball will initially throw very wide, and in this case will contact the cushion before it can arc back to a half-ball line. Place the red about 10 inches (25 cm) and the white about 20 inches (51 cm) away from the side cushion, both being just less than a ball-width off the top cushion. You should be able to make the cannon with a thick half-ball contact. In fact, cannons that are wider than this can be made with a delicate stroke, using a thick half-ball contact and maximum side. Practise playing these cannons from various positions; you will probably be amazed at how easy they are.

Allow for a wide cue ball deflection angle when dealing with an object ball close to a cushion or another ball

Lesson Three

The Cross-cannon

A cannon played across the table when the first object ball is close to a cushion

The problem with cross-cannons such as this one is that they are easy to *see*, but extremely difficult to *play* because the first object ball is so close to the cushion. You have just seen how the cue ball arcs immediately after contact with the object ball. Because of the pace required for these cross-cannons, the cue ball hits the cushion while still arcing, making the angle onto the cushion very difficult to judge. In addition, small changes in contact and pace make a big difference to the angle that the cue ball initially makes with the cushion. In some cases the cue ball will impact the cushion at a slight angle backwards, so the sidespin checks the cue ball.

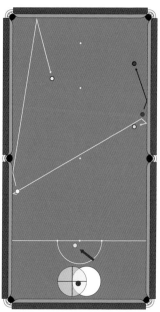

For cross-cannons it is essential that the object ball is not taken too thick and the shot should be played at a true half-ball, or even thinner. With thick contacts, the cue ball will come off the cushion very slowly. You will get a similar effect if you address high on the cue ball, so a slightly below centre address will help to avoid this. Also, if you are in hand, set the angle so that sidespin can be applied to run off the cushion.

This next shot, known as the *cross in-off*, is not a high percentage shot. Only play it as a *shot-to-nothing*, or perhaps for a practice shot to help you to judge the cross-cannon. It is a tough shot, and the cue ball will not come off the side cushion at the same angle on all tables. Although you might find that you have reasonable success with this

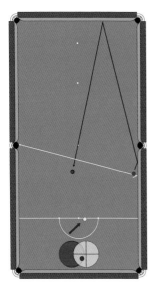

in-off when playing on your practice table, don't be fooled into thinking that it is quite easy to play on all tables. If a double pot red is on, that would usually be a higher percentage shot.

Cross-cannons such as this next one are much more reliable than when the first object ball is very close to the cushion. Notice that the red ball is some distance away from the side cushion, and this means that

with slow or medium paced shots the cue ball will have finished arcing by the time it hits the cushion.

Practise similar shots to the one shown. From hand, it helps to set the cue ball so that a touch of running side is required to make the shot, as this prevents applying any unwanted check side.

Remember
✓ If the first object ball is close to a cushion, play a true half-ball contact, or even thinner than this
✓ Use running side (off the cushion) if the angle permits

Try to avoid
✗ Playing the cross in-off
✗ Using a high address

Lesson Three

The Two-cushion Cannon

A shot played with sidespin to run the cue ball off two cushions in order to make a cannon

This two-cushion cannon recovery shot is played with running side (off the cushion) and is relatively easy if the angle is suitable. It is well worth being on the lookout for this type of cannon, which might give better results than a one-cushion alternative, but the shot needs to be *on* in the first place. It will probably take you a good while before you can recognize when the balls are well positioned for cannons such as this.

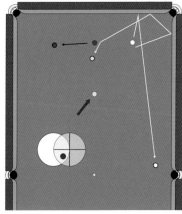

The position shown has the red on the spot and the cue ball on the pyramid spot, with the white level with the red and halfway from the spot to the side cushion. Play the shot with left side, to run off the cushions. Do not hit the white too thick; a true half-ball is sufficient and will help to keep plenty of pace in the cue ball.

This position at the baulk end is one where the two-cushion cannon is a fantastic shot to employ. Of course you could play the 90° screw loser off the white, but that could easily leave the white in baulk. The two-cushion cannon will take the white out of baulk and, providing that you don't hit the shot too hard, should leave a scoring opportunity

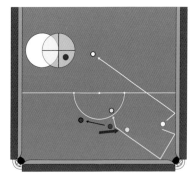

● Lesson Three

off the red. As with all of these two-cushion cannons, the angle has to be suitable for you to play the shot.

The two-cushion cannon can also be employed over longer distances, although it is best if the second object ball is a big target, as is the case here. From this position a)long loser off the red is likely to cause the red to collide with the white, making position uncertain. A far more productive shot is to play the two-cushion cannon, to leave the red near the right corner pocket and the white near the spot. You will probably be amazed at how often you will get a lovely positional outcome off this cannon.

Once you are confident with this shot, when faced with the white in the position shown you might wish to recover it by positioning the red *deliberately* for this two-cushion cannon. This pattern of play can be devastatingly effective.

Remember
✓ Use running side
✓ A true half-ball contact is usually best

Try to avoid
✗ Playing the shot if the angle is not suitable

Shot selection: Looking out for a shot-to-nothing

This position demonstrates how astute shot selection can make a difference to your match-winning potential. There is a possible indirect cannon from red to white, with the white being a big target as it is just off the top cushion. However, this is a tough shot because the cue ball is so far away from the red, which must be contacted extremely finely in order to make the cannon. Also, if you miss the cannon you are likely to leave your cue ball near the left corner pocket.

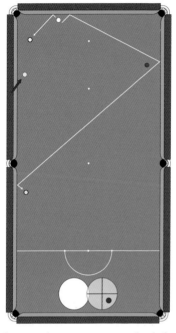

A screw loser off the white is possible, but it is a low percentage shot. The cue ball is a long distance from the white and also quite close to the side cushion, which will affect your cueing.

You might consider a safety shot, making a thin contact on the left side of the white. Whilst this would be an easy shot to play, there is a better option here—a *shot-to-nothing*.

If you assume that you will *miss* the shot, an indirect white to red cannon can be played in such a way to leave the balls safe. Don't play the shot to leave the cue ball close to the red after the cannon, because if you miss you will leave an easy opening for your opponent. By playing with more pace and contacting the white very finely with running side, you will leave a safe position similar to that shown, should you miss the red. At the same time, you would probably create a decent opening if you were to make the cannon. The thin contact on the white will leave it near the left corner pocket, for a possible in-off, and you would also have a fair chance of leaving a scoring shot off the red.

The Indirect Screw Cannon
A cannon played with screw and side to run off one or more cushions

This two-cushion cannon is played with screw and sidespin, to run off the top and side cushions. In the position shown, a run-through cannon is a tough shot because of the risk of the white colliding with the red. However, the two-cushion cannon is a good choice of shot, especially because the red is easy to hit when played this way. There is always the option of playing a similar shot off one cushion, but in this case you would have to use a lot of backspin. Also, the red is more difficult to hit when coming directly from the top cushion.

For this two-cushion cannon, if you over-screw the shot the cue ball will impact the cushion nearer to square-on, so the side will have more effect. If you under-screw the shot, the cue ball will impact the cushion at more of an angle, so the side will take less. Therefore, errors in the amount of screw applied are not too critical. Set the balls as shown and experiment with the shot. You must apply enough sidespin to make the cue ball spin off the two cushions.

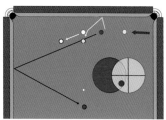

This next shot is one that comes up quite regularly, with the balls *covered* so that a run-through cannon is not possible. The cannon needs to be played indirectly. You have already seen that shots played squarely onto a cushion with check side can give poor results, and nothing is different with this cannon! It will probably feel instinctive to stun the cue ball onto the top cushion using right side, but there is a better way to play the shot. Instead, use screw and left side to run off the top cushion. You might be amazed at how easy the shot is when played this way. Try other cannons from similar positions to see how easy it is to play them using running side off the cushion. When playing this cannon, it is obviously essential that you avoid knocking the red onto the white. Therefore, you might need to play a thin contact but if the position permits use a thick half-ball.

This last cannon is a valuable shot that occurs frequently, especially at the top end. At first glance it might seem as though this position is poor, as the white is too straight for a run-through loser and the pot red would be far from certain. However, an indirect screw cannon is a simple shot that can gather the balls near the left corner pocket.

Set the position shown, although the ball positions do not need to be exact as the cannon can be made from a variety of leaves. Play a crisp screw-back with plenty of left sidespin. A crucial aspect of the shot is to make a 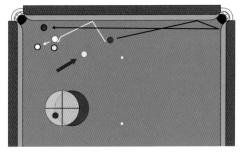 full contact onto the white, in order to leave a white loser. In addition, adjust the red contact so that it catches the right pocket jaw and comes back across the table to meet the other two balls, as shown. Once you are confident with this basic shot practise a variety of cannons from other similar positions.

Remember
✓ Use plenty of running side
✓ Adjust the contact in order to make the shot and leave good position

Try to avoid
✗ Using check side

Concept: The 90° kiss cannon rule

When the angle between all three balls is about a right angle, with the first object ball within about ½ inch (1.3 cm) of a cushion, a true half-ball contact will make the cannon. This is true for shots played between about 30° to the cushion and square-on.

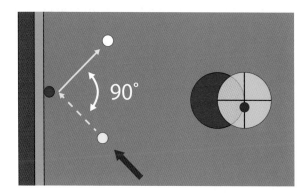

Concept: Using a low address for kiss cannons

If a ball is rolling when it hits a ball that is tight on the cushion, after the kiss it will skid for a while before starting to roll again. The best way to play kiss cannons is to address the cue ball so that on impact with the object ball it is either skidding or carrying an amount of backspin. The cue ball might still skid slightly after the kiss, but will start to roll much more quickly than if it had been played with natural roll.

**It is best to play kiss cannons
by using a low address**

The Kiss Cannon

A double kiss off a ball that is very close to a cushion, in order to make a cannon

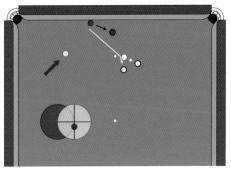

Kiss cannons are beautiful shots that are much easier to play than they look. Although many players avoid playing basic kiss cannons, in favour of attempting much harder shots, don't be afraid of them because you will make quick progress with these shots if you practise them. They are best played with thick contacts and at anything less than half-ball they become more difficult to judge. You will often find that, at less than quarter-ball contacts, there is a danger of not getting the kiss.

The diagram shows a basic kiss cannon and once you have mastered this you can use it to help you judge other kiss cannons. Set the balls as shown, at an approximate right angle and play the cannon. Remember to address below centre; this will help to keep pace in the cue ball after the kiss. Once you get the feel of the shot you might be surprised at how easy it is. Remember to point your cue at the edge of the red.

If the angle is greater than a right angle you will need to point your cue slightly outside the edge of the red, whereas if the angle is less than a right angle you will have to point your cue slightly inside the edge of the red. You will probably need

In case you were wondering…

As the cue ball hits the object ball it is stopped in its tracks. The object ball drives into the cushion rubber, rebounding and hitting the cue ball again. Therefore, there are two definite contacts between the balls. You do not hear the double contact, but it is there.

to experiment with various contacts to be comfortable with these variations in the 90° kiss cannon.

This kiss cannon is a terrific shot to remember and can leave you at the top of the table. Because the cue ball path is less than 30° to the cushion the 90° rule does not hold for this cannon and the angle the cue ball takes will be

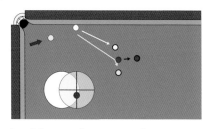

greater than this. Nevertheless, it should not take you too long to get the idea of the shot. If you play the shot correctly, you will leave yourself in prime position. The white needs to be taken slightly thicker than the true half-ball, at least at a thick half-ball.

Usually, kiss cannons should be played over short distances but if the object ball is a big target it is worth having a go at even longer distance kiss cannons. However, the distance from the cue ball to the first object ball should ideally never be large.

Practise this cannon, with the balls as shown, but make sure that the red is about a ball-width off the side cushion so that it is a big target. For these longer distance kiss cannons it is essential that the cue ball is either skidding or carrying backspin when it hits the first object ball.

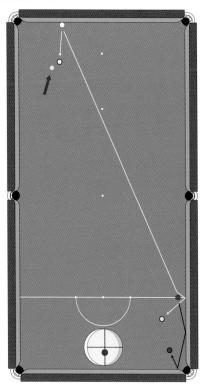

Lesson Three

This last kiss cannon is slightly different from those already discussed because there is no double kiss, just a kiss between the two object balls. Instead of trying to make an angle, deliberately set the cue ball *directly in line* with the red and the white. Aim to hit the red at full-ball, but over this long distance you are almost certain to be slightly inaccurate. The diagrams show the red being hit slightly on the right side, knocking it to the left with the white coming off the top cushion to meet the cue ball. The blue circle shows the approximate position of the kiss between the cue ball and the white. Play the cannon at a slow pace to

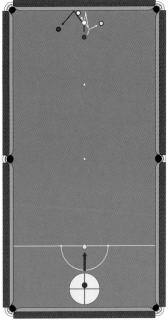

leave the balls at the top end.

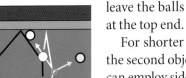

For shorter range cannons, especially with the second object ball close to the cushion, you can employ sidespin to assist the shot. Right side would throw the red to the left and left sidespin would make the cannon in the opposite sense.

Remember
✓ Aim inside the edge of the object ball for angles less than 90°
✓ Aim outside the edge of the object ball for angles greater than 90°
✓ Aim for a full-ball contact, possibly with sidespin, for cannons with the balls in line

Try to avoid
✗ Playing with too much pace

Patterns of play: Cannon moves

By now your game should consist of sequences of shots that fit together to form small scoring patterns. You should have your own preferred methods of scoring in order to make breaks and be able to recognize positions as they arise, with a plan in mind for how to continue your break. You will have committed many different patterns to your memory and as you continue to play billiards you should strive to add even more sequences and moves to your game.

If you work to increase your repertoire of shots and scoring sequences you will become a very difficult player to beat. The following are three cannon set pieces that are worth remembering but there are countless more cannon moves that can also be memorized.

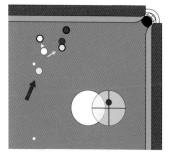

Here, there is a white to red cannon and many league players would play it quite firmly to attempt to push the red to the corner pocket area, probably leaving the white near the top cushion. There is, however, a better way to play the shot, using a set move.

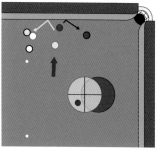

First of all play a slow, thin cannon, from white to red, pushing the red *out of position*, close to the top cushion. Then play a second cannon from red to white, using the top cushion. This second cannon will leave a pot red and nudge the white nearer the spot. This is a lovely move that is often missed, simply because the idea of putting a ball out of position, in this case moving the red to the top cushion, is something that does not come naturally. Of course, the red is only out of position for an instant because the next shot will recover it, and the result of this set piece will usually pay dividends. This idea of taking a ball out of position during a sequence of shots, to gain a better end position, is something that you should be on the lookout for.

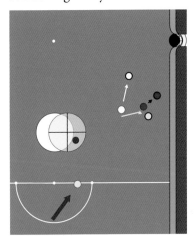

The position shown here is not as straightforward as it first appears. Cannons like this, near baulk, are often trickier than they look. Of course, the scoring shot is easy to make, but you should have a plan on how to move the balls along to the middle pocket area and away from the side cushion. Most league players would play a direct white to red cannon to attempt to leave the balls near the middle pocket. Sometimes an alternative red-cushion-white cannon is played. Both of these shots can easily go wrong, leaving a poor outcome.

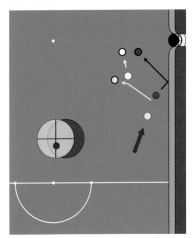

As a general principle, if you are not sure what to do with this type of cannon, it will often pay dividends to play a gentle cannon first and to manoeuvre the balls from there. In this case, if you play a gentle white to red cannon and leave a nice angle between the three balls, you can follow it with another cannon, as shown. There's not too much that can go wrong with the first cannon because even if you hit it too hard you will still have a scoring shot, from either a stun cannon or a cannon using the side cushion. If, by mistake, you happen to nudge the red onto the side cushion, you can employ your knowledge of the 90° kiss cannon rule to continue your break!

Here is a lovely *slip-through* move that often crops up during a game. Play very gently to leave a gap of about a ball-width then, for the second cannon, slip through the balls to leave a pot red. Sometimes it will take more than one cannon to leave a big enough gap; don't worry if this is the case as you will gain an extra two points from any further cannons that you make.

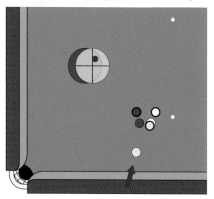

If the gap is a little on the tight side, you can use some check side off the first ball to slip through, making sure to address above centre and to hold the cue lightly.

If the gap between the two object balls is slightly too large, address below centre and use some running side off the first ball; you can also grip the cue slightly harder than usual to help widen the throw off the first object ball.

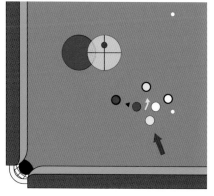

You have now seen a sample of three quite different set moves. As you continue to improve set some time aside to experiment on the table to work out some other set pieces that you can incorporate into your game. Cannons with the object balls between the **D** and the middle pocket area can be surprisingly challenging, so it will be particularly beneficial if you work out methods to manoeuvre the balls from this area.

Lesson Three

Patterns of play: Recovering the white

One important way to improve your overall game is to develop a strategy for recovering the white when it is out of position as it is normally poor billiards to ignore a *dead ball*.

The diagram indicates several white positions and, assuming that you had control of the red, perhaps nicely positioned for a middle-pocket loser, as shown, how would you go about recovering the white from each of these awkward positions? If you can't answer that question, set yourself the task to do some planning along with some experimenting on the practice table, to find patterns of play that work best for you. To help your thought process we'll look at a couple of positions.

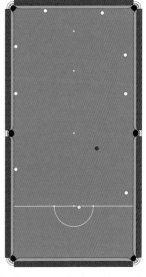

With the white closest to the baulk line on the right side of the table, it would be wise to go after it as soon as possible. There is no easy shot off this white and you should not play losing hazards off the red in the hope to gain a few points before recovering the white. You must bear in mind that one poor positional shot off the red could easily mean the end of your break, so it would be far better to bring the red back to the white *immediately*, in order to carry on your break. Even if you hit the red too hard and it finishes in baulk, you should still have an easy white to red cannon.

With the white on the left side of the top cushion you would need a different strategy. In this case, you *could* play a sequence of red middle-pocket losers to the right middle pocket, safe in the knowledge that by keeping the red on the right side of the table, you would have a red to white cannon if you were to leave the red short. This is quite effective billiards, although not normally the pattern of play that top players would choose. A more attacking style of play is to go after the white at the first opportunity, by manoeuvring the red into your preferred position for a red to white cannon.

Remember that your preferred patterns of play for recovering the white might well be different from those employed by other players. Also, as you improve you will need to adjust these scoring patterns accordingly as you discover more effective methods of break-building.

Once you have worked out strategies for recovering the white, it will also be beneficial if you decide on patterns of play for recovering the red, when it is similarly out of position. Don't underestimate the importance of thinking about these shots and having a plan of action, as it will substantially increase your match-winning potential.

Patterns of play: Dealing with single baulks

White in baulk

It is normally poor billiards to ignore a white that is in baulk and it is usually best to recover it as soon as possible. If the white is in a suitable position, it is best to pot the red at the first opportunity and follow this with an in-off white, to get the white back into play. This pattern of play should lead to a drop cannon, either immediately after the in-off white or, more often, after further white losers to manoeuvre the white into the drop cannon position.

If the white is close to a cushion, as shown here, a cannon is often the best recovery option. In these cases, a red middle-pocket loser is one of the best ways to leave such a cannon. Play the in-off to bring the red close to the baulk line, making sure that you do not double baulk yourself!

A middle-pocket loser is a good shot to employ for recovering the white

There are other patterns of play to leave the red near the baulk line. After two pots off the spot, a quarter-ball to half-ball loser off the red, placed on the centre spot, is a reasonable option. If you are slightly wider than the ideal position you can even take the red in and out of baulk to leave it near the baulk line.

A red loser off the centre spot allows you to leave the red near baulk

If you have the opportunity of playing a cross-loser, you can take the red to the baulk line area by playing the shot more firmly than normal. This is an easy shot to play, but the pattern does not occur too often because you would normally need a reasonably straight pot red off the spot in order to get into position for a cross-loser.

Also, pyramid losers, long-range losers, and sometimes even short jennies can all be used to bring the red close to the baulk line.

It is easy to leave the red near the baulk line from a cross-loser

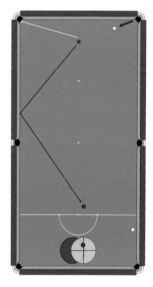

You might also find yourself faced with a long-distance cannon, although this is not the *best* way to recover the white as the positional aspect is risky. Nevertheless, after a second pot off the spot you might leave either a direct, or perhaps an indirect cannon, such as the one shown here. A cannon using the side or baulk cushions might offer a better chance of leaving good position than a direct cannon.

**A long-distance cannon
can be risky**

If the white is a big target it is sometimes better to play this cannon rather than the difficult long loser (sometimes called a *raker),* when the red is in the awkward position inside the shaded area. This area of the table is sometimes referred to as *no-man's land.*

**A multiple-cushion cannon might
be a better option than a raker**

Lesson Three

Red in baulk

The red is more difficult to recover than the white because you are limited to playing losing hazards off the white. Keep in mind that a middle-pocket loser off the white, in order to leave it near baulk, is a risky shot on a table

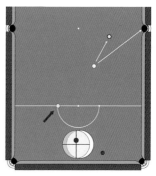

> **In case you were wondering…**
>
> It used to be deemed ungentlemanly conduct if you potted your opponent's white and it is a bizarre fact that many people will still apologize for potting their opponent's ball, even though they meant to do so!

with an inconsistent top cushion as you might inadvertently double baulk yourself. Of course, you might have the option of potting the white and then playing a double baulk, which might be a reasonable alternative.

A pot white / double baulk sequence might be a reasonable option

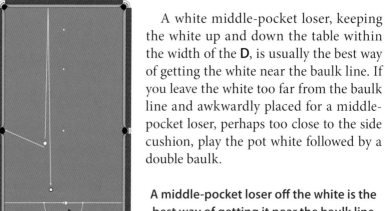

A white middle-pocket loser, keeping the white up and down the table within the width of the **D**, is usually the best way of getting the white near the baulk line. If you leave the white too far from the baulk line and awkwardly placed for a middle-pocket loser, perhaps too close to the side cushion, play the pot white followed by a double baulk.

A middle-pocket loser off the white is the best way of getting it near the baulk line

Patterns of play: Leaving a double baulk

Leaving a *good* double baulk will put the odds in your favour for an easy opening, so it is worth being mindful of some of the key aspects to consider when playing to leave a double baulk.

You might not always be able to predict the final positions of the balls accurately, when playing to leave a double baulk. Here, it is vital to make certain of the double baulk, but you can not guarantee to leave the balls in a decent scoring position for your next visit to the table (assuming that your opponent fails to escape from the double baulk).

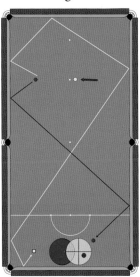

From time to time you will be faced with positions that are even more challenging than this one. Bear in mind that you should never take a significant risk with a double baulk as a failed double baulk attempt can leave your opponent an easy opening. From these awkward positions, consider playing a single baulk, ideally leaving one ball near the top cushion. Remember that a good single baulk can be more effective than a poor double baulk, and certainly far better than a failed attempt at a double baulk!

If the balls are situated so that you *can* control the positional aspect accurately, there are certain guidelines that can assist you to gain the upper hand. It is better to leave yourself a red loser rather than a pot, because from most in-offs you will have a decent chance of gaining good position to continue your break. If you leave yourself a difficult pot your opponent will probably play a safety miss, hoping that you miss the pot. Your opponent might also play a safety miss if you leave an *easy* pot, if the position is such that they judge that you are unlikely to get into a scoring position from this pot. Where possible, leave your cue ball away from the red, as this makes it more difficult for your opponent to make a cannon. Also, do not leave either ball too close to a pocket because this will give your opponent a good opportunity of scoring. Remember that balls in the corner pocket area will be easy targets. Any ball left close to a side cushion is also a big target because it will be extremely easy for your opponent to spoil the position by playing a fast shot off the top cushion.

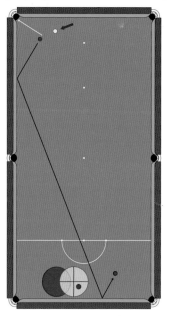

After potting the white, bear in mind that you don't have to play the double baulk immediately. Sometimes it will pay to be patient and manoeuvre the balls into a better position. One pattern of play that can be quite effective is to play a red loser, *deliberately* putting the red into baulk, and then a safety miss to double baulk your opponent. From the position shown here, it is a relatively easy matter to play in-off the red to leave it in baulk. Of course you could leave the red in baulk from many other starting positions, such as from a middle-pocket loser played with more pace than normal. After leaving the red in baulk it will usually be a simple matter to play a controlled safety miss in order to leave an effective double baulk.

This diagram shows a well played safety miss because the cue ball finishes in a position that blocks the opponent's path to the red (off the side cushion), while leaving a reasonable potting angle on the red for your next visit. Although it is usually better to leave yourself a red loser rather than a pot, from this position it can be quite effective to block the side cushion path to the red.

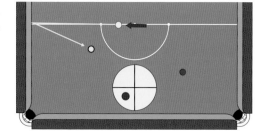

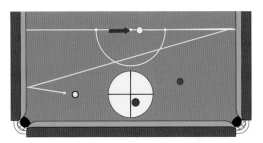

An alternative way of playing a double baulk would be to play twice across the table, leaving yourself a red loser as shown. Although this is a better scoring position, it would be quite easy for your opponent to spoil this by playing with sidespin off the left side cushion, hitting the red.

This last diagram shows a screw shot to bring the red around the table into baulk. Notice how the cue ball has been set at an angle, so that the red finishes a reasonable distance away from it. If the shot had been set for a straight screw-back the cue ball and the red would have finished close together, possibly leaving a good chance of a cannon for your opponent.

When faced with a double baulk situation you will often have to improvise, so remember to practise achieving double baulks from various positions.

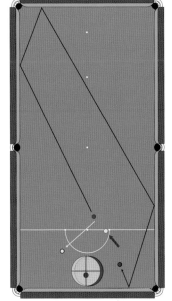

Remember
✓ Try to leave an in-off red
✓ Leave the cue ball and red well apart
✓ After potting your opponent's white, you might want to consider playing a red loser, deliberately putting the red into baulk, and then playing a safety miss

Try to avoid
✗ Leaving balls over a pocket
✗ Leaving balls near a side cushion

Patterns of play: Dealing with double baulks

There are various ways of tackling double baulks, but remember that you don't *have* to attempt to score or even to disturb the balls at all. If your opponent has an easy red loser to play, it is usually best to attempt to spoil that position. However, if you judge that your opponent will probably miss the shot, play a safety miss by aiming out of baulk to leave your cue ball in a safe position. Also, if your opponent is faced with a pot red with a tough positional aspect, so that it is exceptionally difficult to get the cue ball away from the baulk area, you might be better off playing a safety miss.

This shot, played across the table with sidespin, is the most common method of getting out of a double baulk. You will gain a slight geometrical advantage by setting the cue ball away from the cushion you will hit, so that you can play as parallel to the baulk line as possible. However, many players prefer to place the cue ball as near as possible to the side cushion that they will hit, making it slightly easier to hit a point on the side cushion with accuracy. Play with the amount of side that is required to make the shot; in this case about maximum sidespin.

Don't play the shot too hard because, in this case, the cue ball will bed into the cushion and *square-off,* not coming into baulk as much. Shots that require maximum sidespin should be played at a slow to moderate pace. Of course if you don't need maximum sidespin to make the shot you might decide to play it firmly, particularly if you are trying to move a ball and spoil your opponent's position.

There is another way to play double baulk shots off the side cushion when they don't *require* maximum sidespin. Instead of aiming for a point just outside of baulk and varying the spin, you can vary the aim point on the side cushion whilst always using maximum spin. Which method you use will depend on your personal preference.

This three-cushion escape has already been mentioned when describing the advantages of using multiple cushions. Although tables and cushions vary, you should have a clear idea of how a three-cushion shot will play on your practice table, then you can adapt to different conditions. To get different cue ball paths, keep the cue ball at the same position in the **D** and vary the aim point on the side cushion. For this, it is very useful to look at where your cue passes over the baulk corner pocket. It is certainly worth experimenting with this shot to attempt to make cannons from various double baulk positions.

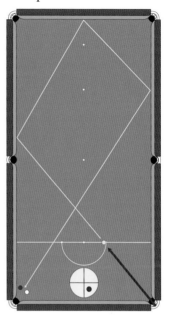

As with all of these double baulk shots, success depends on knowledge

In case you were wondering…

Players of *three-cushion billiards* often employ numeric systems which make use of diamond-shaped markings on the cushion rails of their pocketless tables. The shot shown here is a specific example of one such system in action. That particular system is often called the *Corner-5* system.

and practice. Even so, when you come to an unfamiliar table, the cue ball path will be slightly different from that on your practice table. Try to make a mental note of whether the table is playing *short* (striking the side cushion first) or *long* (striking the baulk cushion first). For example, for the shot shown, if the cue ball misses the cannon by hitting the baulk cushion a couple of ball-widths away from the corner pocket, remember that the cushions are playing two balls long and you will need to aim nearer to the middle pocket for any further cannons like this.

When the target is near the middle of the baulk cushion, you will need to miss the middle pocket on your way around the angles, so this is a challenging shot to play. Surprisingly, it isn't too critical where you choose to set the cue ball, although start your practice from the position shown. Aim for about halfway down the side cushion with maximum running side, making sure not to hit the *left* side cushion too close to the middle pocket, as this might cause you to hit the *right* middle pocket jaws.

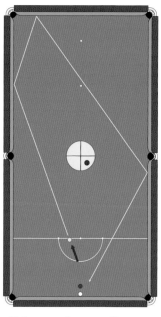

Finally, you will often have the option of a one-cushion cannon, using only the top cushion. You have already seen that when playing square-on to cushions any applied

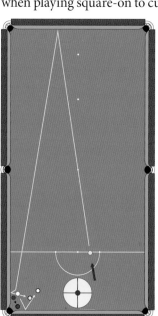

sidespin will have a large effect. In this case, because you are not playing directly off an object ball, as long as you concentrate on *not* applying any sidespin, you will have a reasonable chance of making a cannon. With these one-cushion shots you can use the spots to help you hit the target. For example, if you place the cue ball with the left edge midway between the middle and right spots of the **D**, and aim over the centre spot, you will get very close to the baulk corner pocket. Experiment from various cue ball positions, aiming over the centre, pyramid and the billiard spots, to see what results you get. Memorize the positions that you feel are useful.

Shot selection: Safety options from a double baulk

Faced with this double baulk, you have
several options. As with all double
baulks, you will have to weigh up the
risk, versus the reward. If you think
your opponent will most probably
make the 90° screw loser, you should
attempt a cannon, but you will have
to bear in mind that the red and white
are too far apart for this cannon to be
a high percentage shot.

Alternatively, you might think that your opponent is more likely to
miss the in-off, in which case you will probably attempt a safety shot.
Whenever you play a safety shot, attempt to leave your cue ball in the
most difficult place for a cannon. You know that a ball positioned near
a cushion can be a big target, so avoid leaving your cue ball in an easy
scoring position for a cannon. Look at the angles from which your
opponent is likely to attempt a cannon and leave your cue ball in the
most awkward place possible.

Here is another double baulk and another decision that you will
have to make, based on risk versus reward. Do you think that your

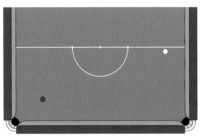

opponent can pot the red and
leave a scoring shot off the red
when it is spotted? If so, you
might decide to attempt to move
the red. There's not much chance
of making a cannon, so the best
you can hope for is to shift the
red to a worse position. If you

think that your opponent is unlikely to leave much off the pot red,
you could consider a safety shot. In this case, be careful where you
leave your cue ball; for example, the left side of the table would not
be a good position because after a stun pot red your opponent would
have a reasonable chance of a cannon.

Lesson Three

This double baulk is a straightforward one to negotiate. Although you could make a cannon, you are more likely to miss it and at the same time leave your opponent with a simple opening shot. You can see that there is no easy shot for your opponent, so a safety shot is the best option here. Interestingly, unlike many

other cue sports, in billiards a good safety shot will leave the odds fairly even as to who scores first. For your safety shot you should bear in mind that the red is a big target for a cannon, so make sure that you don't leave your cue ball in a position that allows a yellow to red cannon. For example, you could decide to leave the cue ball on the right side of the table, between the baulk line and the middle pocket and as close to the cushion as possible. If you do this, a cross-cannon from red to yellow would be an extremely tough shot and any cannon using multiple cushions, either off the red or the yellow, would be far from certain. You would probably force your opponent into playing a safety shot.

From this last position, your opponent has a reasonable opportunity of a pot red to either the right middle or top pocket. The other scoring possibilities are an in-off into the top left pocket or a screw loser into the left baulk pocket, but both of these are low percentage shots.

Instead of attempting a low probability cannon, you could play a delicate safety miss to spoil the position for your opponent. By bridging *over* the red and gently pushing your cue ball out of baulk, you could block the pot red to one (or both) of the pockets. However, don't leave the red and yellow too close together to allow your opponent the opportunity of a cushion-first cannon.

The Cushion-first Cannon

A cannon played off a cushion before hitting the first object ball, in order to make an angle for the shot

Cushion-first cannons are not always obvious shots, but they can sometimes be much easier to play than other alternatives.

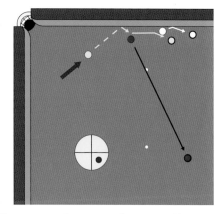

Practise making the cannon with the red between 1¼ to 1¾ ball-widths off the cushion. Right sidespin will be needed in order to get between the red and the cushion.

Once you are confident with this, experiment with other *cue ball* positions. When the cue ball is nearer the top cushion it will come away from the cushion after contact with the red. Also, as the cue ball is moved further from the cushion there will come a point beyond which you can't get under the red and, once again, the cue ball will diverge from the cushion.

In case you were wondering…

In the game of three-cushion billiards, a shot similar to this is often called a *ticky*.

Now move the *red* slightly nearer the cushion. It becomes more of a challenge to get under the red and the cue ball will diverge from the cushion. The nearer the red is to the top cushion the more the cue ball will diverge.

Finally, attempt cannons with the red about two ball-widths or slightly more away from the cushion. A naturally rolling cue ball will come away from the cushion but it *is* possible to make the cue ball travel parallel to the cushion by playing reasonably firmly with a high address. The cue ball will then stun off the red to make the cannon.

Lesson Three

This next cannon is a useful one to try, especially as it is a shot that is often overlooked, and of course *you can't play the shot if you don't see the shot!* If you imagine the cue ball to be tight on the left cushion you should see the half-ball cannon without any difficulty, so it will be beneficial for you to look at the shot from that angle, until you get used to this type of cannon. Address slightly below

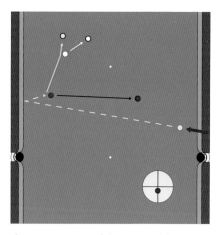

centre to make the cannon. In order to gain confidence and become proficient at cannons such as this, you will need to repeat them time after time. If you are unsure of the angle, walk around to the other side of the table to look at the shot from that perspective. This type of shot is sometimes referred to as a *back-heel cannon.*

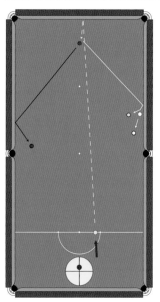

Here, the red is on the spot and a cushion-first cannon is a good option, anything else being a tough shot. Set the cue ball in about the same position that you would use for a long loser off an object ball on the centre spot and play to just miss the red on the way to the top cushion. Don't play the shot too hard because you want the cue ball to be rolling naturally by the time it hits the red. If you play the shot with too much pace the cue ball will be skidding when it hits the red, after impacting the cushion, and this will cause a wider throw off the red. Address above centre for long-distance cushion-first cannons, as it helps to avoid imparting sidespin.

Cannons such as this are easiest when the first object ball is on, or very close to, the cushion and also when the second one is a big target, near a cushion. Play with running side to hit the cushion just before the white. You might be surprised at how easy this cannon is, as there is quite a large margin for error with this shot.

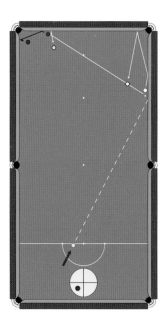

To get the cue ball to hit nearer to the centre of the top cushion, place it further to the right. Conversely, to make a cannon near the corner pocket, place the cue ball on the left spot of the **D**. This will probably not be intuitive and you might feel that you are moving the cue ball the wrong way!

This next cushion-first cannon is a useful one to know and much better than playing a low percentage pot red. Again, this cannon is rarely played because it is seldom recognized as a good shot option.

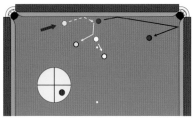

Play with right side and screw, to hit the cushion before the red. This is a delicate shot, so don't hit it too hard. As the cue ball will hit the cushion at a very acute angle, the screw effect that you saw in lesson two (*screwing off a cushion*) does not apply.

Remember
✓ Be on the lookout for an opportunity of a cushion-first cannon
✓ You might find it useful to walk around to the other side of the table in order to look at the cushion-first cannon from that perspective

The Cushion-first Loser

An in-off played off a cushion before hitting the object
ball in order to make a suitable angle

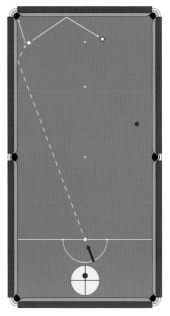

You will probably be wary about
attempting cushion-first losers, such
as this one, but they are useful shots to
have in your repertoire.

Set the balls as shown, with the
white level with the billiard spot and
in line for a straight pot if the cue ball
were positioned on the right spot of
the **D**. Make a small chalk mark on the
front face of the side cushion, 24 inches
(61 cm) away from the top cushion.
Play the shot without sidespin and *aim*
directly for the chalk mark. Of course,
the cue ball will hit the cushion just
before the mark, making the correct
angle for the in-off.

Practise the shot, addressing the cue
ball as shown, until you are comfortable
with it, before experimenting with other white positions close to this
one. Adjust the cue ball position in the **D** in order to make the shot.
For example, if the white were slightly further from the side cushion,
you would need to move the cue ball to the left side of the **D** and when
nearer the side cushion, to the right.

You might find it useful to walk to the side cushion area and look at
the shot from that perspective, so that you can imagine playing a thick
half-ball loser from a point on the side cushion. You should be able to
see where the cue ball needs to hit the side cushion to make the shot.

So far you have not used sidespin, but you will get a slight advantage
by playing with *cushion sidespin*. Although this is *check side* (off the

cushion) and you have already seen that it is normally not a good idea to check off cushions, in this case the angle of approach is so acute that the side has virtually no effect on the rebound angle. The side will remain on the cue ball after contact with both the cushion and the object ball and should spin the cue ball in off the pocket jaws.

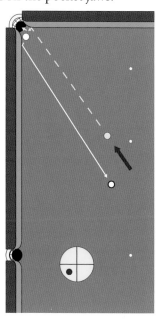

When the white is very close to the pocket jaws it is usually advantageous to play an in-off, if possible, rather than potting the white. In the position shown you could always pot the white, but that would limit the size of your break. Nevertheless, in the final stages of a match if you feel that the in-off is too risky, it might be best to play a pot white followed by either a series of red hazards, or a double baulk.

As a very rough guide, when the white is in the jaws of the pocket, you can often make an in-off if the total space either side of the white adds up to about the width of a ball. So if the white were tight against one pocket jaw, the gap on the other side should be at least a ball-width, for the in-off to be possible. In the diagram, the white is a quarter of a ball-width off the side cushion jaw, with a gap of three-quarters of a ball-width on the other side, so the in-off can be made.

Play the in-off from the position shown. Remember to get running side on the cue ball to get inside the pocket jaws. Try the shot from different cue ball and white positions.

Remember
- ✓ You might find it useful to walk around to the other side of the table in order to look at the cushion-first loser from that perspective
- ✓ Use sidespin and/or cue ball positioning to make the in-off
- ✓ If the white is in the pocket jaws use plenty of running side

Lesson Three

Lesson Three Summary

- If the object ball is awkwardly placed, just above the centre spot, play a slow long loser from hand to leave the object ball near the pyramid spot.

- For slow, naturally rolling shots, don't adjust for the nap when playing *with* the nap but make a small allowance when playing diagonally *against* the nap.

- When playing forcing losers from hand try to leave the object ball away from cushions—you might need to adjust the cue ball position to achieve this.

- Use running side for cushion cannons.

- For long-distance cushion cannons always consider the target size, and it is often best to use multiple cushions.

- Kiss cannons are easy to play if the angle between the three balls is about 90°.

- If the white is in baulk, try to recover it at the earliest opportunity.

- If the red is in baulk, try to recover it but bear in mind the option of a pot white / double baulk pattern.

- Cannons and in-offs played cushion-first are useful recovery shots, but you need to learn to recognize them.

Appendix A
Making the best use of your time

As with most sports, to make the quickest progress you should follow a training schedule. If you spend nearly all of your time on one specific aspect of the game, perhaps just practising with a friend, you certainly won't improve as quickly as you could do. Similarly, if you devote all of your time to solo practice you will find it difficult to compete under match conditions and when you eventually play on an unfamiliar table you will be at a huge disadvantage. Although you have the will to win, do you have the will to *prepare* to win?

How to manage your practice

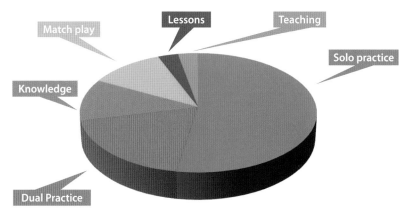

The chart is an example of some important aspects of billiards that need attention from time to time. You will know your own strengths and weaknesses and with these in mind you should manage your practice accordingly and devise a schedule that is appropriate for your game, always of course within the time that you have available.

During your practice, set your own targets but try to make sure that they are realistic and achievable while still requiring some effort.

Remember that enjoyment is one of the keys to improvement, so if you don't feel like completing a specific practice routine, then switch to something else.

Solo practice

You will unquestionably find that you become a more accomplished player if you complete a substantial amount of solo practice, so this aspect is discussed in more detail in a separate section, immediately after discussing how best to manage your practice time.

Dual practice

You should endeavour to play practice matches with a friend or colleague. You might want to handicap these matches if you are at significantly different standards, so that the matches are meaningful to both of you. It is usually best to use a changeable handicap system that allows both of you to win an equal number of matches. For example, with a 200-up game you might start with a handicap so that you need to score 200 and your playing partner only 180. Should you win, perhaps change the handicap so that your playing partner only needs 170 to win the next game, and so on. Another method of handicapping is to add a number of points to each break, or perhaps each visit, that one player makes. So taking the above example, you could add one point to every break that your colleague makes and, depending on the outcome, adjust this handicap for your next game. Of course, it is not so relevant to handicap shorter duration matches as these will always allow the weaker player to win an occasional game.

When you play a game with a friend record the number of visits to the table so that you can take the average score for each visit. Your average (your total score divided by your number of completed visits) is the best way of determining your standard and your improvement. These recorded results will encourage you to practise and improve. It might be tempting to use your highest break as a measure of your improvement, but it is your long-term average that gives a true measure of performance, so don't be disheartened if you do not improve on your highest break for a while.

During your games make a conscious effort to remember any unfamiliar shots or things that went wrong, so that you can experiment with them and discuss them with your practice partner. Try to set some time aside to do this at the end of your matches.

Knowledge

One of the most underrated methods of improving is to increase your knowledge and to keep reading, learning and thinking about the game. It is surprising how much this will help you advance.

One way to increase your knowledge is to watch top players and try to work out what improvements you can make to your game. When watching good players in action, avoid focussing on the state of the game or the size of a particular break being made. Focus instead on individual shots and be especially on the lookout for positions that you have trouble with, making a mental note of how they are handled. Before a player takes each shot you might want to visualize what you would play from that position and after the shot compare your choice of shot with what was played. You might be able to incorporate that particular shot or pattern into your game, but remember that your patterns of play will need to be within your capabilities.

Don't forget that the *englishBilliards.org* website has many instructional videos along with videos of complete billiards matches, so that you can watch how some of the top players play the game.

Match play

One of the best ways to improve is to join a local league or play in competitions. Competing will give you feedback on areas of your game that need improvement. You will be able to watch other players and learn from their game, giving you the drive and determination to become a better player. You will also learn to adapt to different tables and playing conditions.

Lessons

If you are serious about becoming the best player that you possibly can be you will need to take lessons from time to time. No matter how much effort you put in to developing your game you will never reach your potential without learning some of the finer aspects of billiards from a knowledgeable player. Of course billiards is not unique in this respect, but because of the depth and complexity inherent in the game you will find that lessons will probably give more improvement than in many other sports or games.

Teaching

If you are able to pass on some of *your* knowledge to a player who is also learning the game, then do so. Not only will it promote the game, it will almost certainly help you to improve. For example, you might need to explain the reasons why you are playing a particular shot and exactly how to play it. The very act of doing this will cause you to think more about your game and, surprisingly perhaps, this will often result in further improvement in your own play.

How to allocate your solo practice time

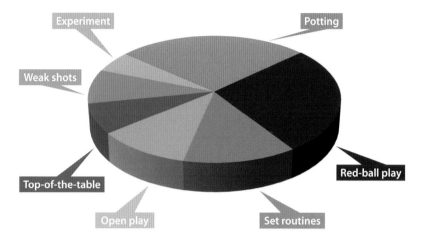

Having looked at some ways to manage your practice time, it is worth looking at how to get the most out of your solo practice. The chart shows how a top player might spend solo practice time, but of course you will want to decide for yourself how to manage your own solo practice sessions. You should know the parts of your game that need the most improvement and allocate more time to these aspects. The most important point is that it should be fun—there is no use repeating shot after shot if you are not enjoying it! Keep a record of your progress and breaks to measure your improvement.

If you have had a considerable amount of practice recently, perhaps using a schedule similar to that shown in the chart, you might want to focus *all* of your practice on one specific part of your game. This type of focussed practice is extremely beneficial when learning new skills. For example, if you feel that you need to improve your skills at escaping from double baulks, some intensive practice at these shots will yield better results than fragmented practice. Make sure though, that you don't switch to focussed practice until you are comfortable with your general form.

Potting

Good potting is essential for advanced billiards so spend a substantial amount of time on this along with improving your cue action. Amongst other things, this will help you to stand up to pressure in a match. There are three main aspects of potting that are particularly important for billiards.

Firstly, you must be proficient at potting the red at the spot end. Perhaps surprisingly, most players will find that a high percentage of breaks finish with a missed pot off the spot, so make sure that you do not disregard this crucial aspect of the game. A good practice routine is to see how many consecutive pots off the spot you can make; you will almost certainly find this task much harder than you might think.

Secondly, you should be proficient at potting the red into a middle pocket when playing from hand. Whether this is to leave a middle cross-loser or to take the cue ball to the top of the table, you should be confident of making the pot and gaining good position consistently.

Lastly, it is essential to work on your long potting and certain aspects of your technique. For example, you might feel that you are moving on the shot or that your timing needs some adjustment. One pot that occurs quite frequently when out of position is a stun pot red when it is just past a middle pocket (so that you can't play an in-off). You might want to practise this pot to leave the cue ball on a line for the middle cross-loser. Also, make sure you practise other pots that you are not comfortable with; perhaps when the cue ball is tight against a cushion or some exceptionally long-distance pots.

Red-ball play

Whatever your standard, allocate a significant proportion of your practice time to red-ball play. Even when you become quite proficient at all aspects of billiards your hazard game will need to be strong in order to control the balls. Don't disregard some of the seemingly easier aspects of red-ball play such as middle-pocket losers as, although these shots might be easy to make individually, to use them as a match-winning force you will need to be able to play a sequence of them. At the same time, don't be disheartened if you find this difficult to do, as even top players find this a challenge. However, what you *must* be able to do is to control the red's path, making sure that you always leave a scoring position if you get the pace wrong.

Set routines
You should spend some time practising making breaks from set positions. Use some of the positions from this book along with making up your own set routines. These should sometimes require you to make one or more challenging shots before you can go on to make a break, as this can be a rewarding and valuable way to practise.

Open play
From time to time you should simply practise making breaks from random positions. Choose a ball for the cue ball, take all three balls in your hand, place them on the bed of the table and roll them all quickly against a cushion. Once they come to rest, play from the resulting position. Imagine being in a match, so don't forget that you should also practise playing safe if that is the best option. You can repeat this exercise or, after you miss a shot, use the other cue ball and continue from there. This will give you experience at attempting difficult opening shots, similar to those that you will be faced with in a match.

Another method for improving your open play is to play a simulated match against yourself. For example, if you think you can average five points per visit, record your points and also give your simulated opponent five points for every visit that you make.

Be self-critical with your shot selection. If your choice of shot is poor but you achieve a nice positional outcome due to luck, do not be fooled into thinking that you have played a good shot! Put the balls back and take time to work out a way to get a successful result consistently.

Top-of-the-table
Although this book does not include specific top-of-the-table patterns, you might already have some knowledge about this part of the game. If you are having difficulty with a particular move, work on that position for a while rather than always attempting to make breaks.

Weak shots

Part of your solo practice time should be spent practising your weak shots, whatever you think they might be. If you feel that you are especially poor at one particular shot then practise it until you are more confident with it, ideally making it your new favourite shot. To begin with it will be necessary to repeat it time after time, until you are confident that you can make it consistently. This part of your practice will develop your motor skills to play the shot. However, after achieving a reasonable standard at an individual shot, you should then group it with other shots. For example, if there were five or six shots that you were struggling with, but you now feel that you are reasonably proficient at them, play them in sequence. You could then repeat this sequence a number of times, recording your results. By practising a sequence of different shots you will add a small amount of pressure to each shot and you can measure your improvement by looking at your results.

Experiment

Set some time aside to experiment and try out some new shots as this can be great fun! During your games make a conscious effort to remember any unfamiliar shots that arose or things that went wrong, so that you can experiment with them at the practice table. You should also experiment with sidespin application to find out the technique that works best for you in order that you are able to apply the maximum amount of spin. Don't be afraid to miscue from time to time as you find out the limits of the cue ball address. A set of spotted balls will help you to see the spin on the cue ball.

Appendix B

Technique

This book is aimed at players who already have the fundamentals of stance and cue delivery. Nevertheless, everyone is ultimately limited by their technique. This appendix provides a summary of some of the critical aspects of the techniques required to achieve good cueing.

We do many things in everyday life, such as eating and walking, without consciously thinking about them, and these skills are so ingrained that we can do them without paying attention. As you progress with billiards you should aim to build up your knowledge along with your repertoire of shots and patterns of play so that you don't need to *think* about what presents itself on the table; you should know the shot and the pattern that you wish to play from the position you are left. Similarly, your cue delivery should be natural and practised so that the motor skills required to deliver the cue are intrinsic. Strive to play naturally without thinking about it at the conscious level. Of course, you will sometimes be presented with a position that confuses you; perhaps you will not be sure whether to try to score or to play a safety shot. In each of these cases you will need to work out a strategy and take more time choosing your shot.

Decide what to play

Before you get down for your shot, be absolutely clear as to what you are going to play and how you are going to play it. You might need to stand back from the shot and analyse it. If you begin thinking about altering the shot when you are about to play it, you should stop, stand up, and begin your preparation again.

Walk into the shot

Now, starting from behind the cue ball, walk *into* the shot, looking along the line that you are going to play. As you get down to address the cue ball, initially look at the object ball and the line of aim that you need.

Get into your stance

Just before you are fully down on the shot point your cue at the aim point on the cue ball. Now look back and forth from cue ball to object ball in order to line up the shot, whilst completing your preliminary strokes (known as feathering). At this point you should be in your stance. Having a solid stance is fundamental to playing good billiards and your stance should allow you to keep still on the shot, feel comfortable, and deliver the cue in a straight line.

Use the appropriate feathering

The amount and type of preliminary strokes very much depend on your personal preference and you will need to experiment with different techniques to find out what works for you. Two to five preliminary strokes should normally be enough. Some players prefer evenly sized preliminary strokes and others either increase or decrease the amount of cue action in order to prepare for the shot. Most top players try to use a constant number of preliminary strokes for the majority of shots as this tends to help with a rhythm of play and aids concentration.

Pause *before* the backswing

At the end of these preliminary strokes it is usually best to pause, with the cue pointing at the cue ball at the point where you mean to hit it, before starting the backswing. At this moment, your tip should be very close to the cue ball.

Pause *after* the backswing

Your cue and cue arm have a natural cadence in just the same way that a pendulum or a garden swing has. If you try to go against your natural rhythm, then, to some extent, you will lose timing. For example, if you use a very quick backswing and delivery without any pause at the end of the backswing you will be effectively fighting against the rhythm of the shot and will not get as much spin or screw on the cue ball. If you try to push a garden swing forwards when it is travelling backwards you will get the same effect; it will not want to move against the natural timing. However, give it a push as it is just about to begin moving downwards and it will accelerate nicely. Therefore, it is essential to have at least some pause at the end of the backswing, as the cue direction reverses.

Use a smooth cue action

As the most common stroke in billiards is the losing hazard it is extremely important to be able to get the cue ball rolling naturally before it hits the object ball. Many of the strokes played from hand will be half-ball shots and you must concentrate on the smoothness of your cue action to achieve a consistent natural angle deflection. To get a half-ball loser the quality of the stroke must be such that the cue ball is truly rolling on impact with the object ball. Jerky or punchy cue actions can cause the cue ball to be skidding on impact with the object ball and to take a wider path than the natural angle. One of the most difficult things to master is how to strike the cue ball sweetly, with a long follow-through, getting the tip to grip the cue ball.

You should also use the appropriate amount of backswing for the shot. For example, to play a forcing loser you will need a long backswing but for a gentle cannon you should move your grip up the cue, move your bridge closer to the cue ball and use a very short backswing. For shots in between use the length of backswing that you need, and no more.

Deliver the cue along a straight line

As you pause at the end of your backswing you should be aligned on the shot, aiming correctly and be set up, ready to deliver your cue in a straight line. By now you should have decided what shot to play and the line of aim; now is not the time to change anything. For example, trying to apply that extra bit of side at this late stage can end in disaster. Deliver the cue through the line that you have chosen. If you try to adjust your cue delivery at the last minute it will often end in a poorly played shot. A late twist of the wrist, adjustment of aim or address should be avoided. Test yourself by playing a straight pot off the billiard spot with your eyes *closed*. When you are all set to play the shot, close both eyes and deliver the cue. You should be able to do this. You might want to try this practice routine with other more difficult shots, such as in-offs from longer distances. You will probably be surprised at how many you can make.

Make a good follow-through

For many billiards shots it is absolutely essential that you concentrate on pushing through and trying to accelerate through the cue ball, with *as long a follow-through as you can manage*. You will need to hold the cue lightly in order to do this, as a tight grip will hinder the movement of your cue. With a long follow-through the tip will remain in contact with the cue ball for as long as possible and you will get more *action* on the cue ball. This protracted follow-through is particularly critical when imparting maximum sidespin. Top players employ this technique to great effect and the extra spin that they impart by pushing smoothly and crisply through the cue ball makes shots such as spinning run-throughs much easier to make.

> **In case you were wondering...**
>
> As your tip hits the cue ball your cue will *decelerate*, so it is actually impossible to accelerate through the cue ball, and you will, at best, achieve near to a constant cue speed at impact.

Appendix C
Table conditions

One of the biggest challenges in billiards is to be able to adapt to various playing conditions. You will probably have favourite table conditions, especially if you are used to practising on one specific table. Bear in mind that you will rarely play on tables that are similar to your own practice table and that playing in local leagues is one of the best ways to improve your ability to adapt to different conditions. Also, it is important that you devote a percentage of your practice time to playing on a variety of tables. This will help you get the feel of how tables with different cloths and cushion responsiveness affect the various shots, and this will help prepare you for your matches. Also, you might want to change the smoothness of the nap and the speed of your practice table by brushing and ironing the cloth.

Do not be disheartened if you feel that you are having difficulty adapting to different tables, as this is a skill that can be learnt. Top players find this aspect of the game extremely challenging, but they have usually spent many years playing in leagues and experiencing such things as different venues, tables, cloths and lighting, so that they seem to adapt to the table conditions remarkably quickly. Nevertheless, they still have to adapt their play to suit the conditions.

At the beginning of a match you will need to find out how the table is playing. At this stage, don't play shots too delicately; make sure that you score. Once you become familiar with the conditions you can play shots to finer limits. As the match progresses you will need to analyse the table and adapt accordingly. For example, you might have to allow for unpredictable cushions.

Speed
The specific make of table, the atmospheric conditions and the type and condition of the cushion rubbers and the cloth, all have an impact on the speed of the table. The fastest tables are normally located in a

warm and dry environment, with a worn or fine cloth that has been brushed and ironed.

How fast a table is playing is generally measured in lengths of the table; that is, by rolling a ball firmly to the top cushion and seeing how many times it travels up and down (counting the roll to the top cushion as one length). A standard speed is between about four and a half to five lengths. Less than this would be considered slow, although it would be unusual to find a table that ran less than four lengths. Anything more than about five lengths would be considered fast.

Until you are familiar with the speed of the table, make sure that you don't over-hit shots, such as double baulking yourself off a middle-pocket loser. In this particular case, it would be far better to leave the object ball short than to knock it into baulk. You might also play on recently recovered tables that have reasonably slow cushions but a fast bed and these conditions can be quite a challenge to adapt to.

> **In case you were wondering…**
>
> If a table is playing very slowly it is possible to increase the speed significantly by wiping a wet cloth along each of the cushion faces. This is not usually a good idea because it causes the balls to bounce.

Also, a table that is fitted with under-table heaters can present a challenge. These heaters are usually about 5°C warmer than the ambient temperature, so after about a day or so the woollen cloth dries out sufficiently and this reduced humidity increases the speed of the table significantly, sometimes even up to six lengths.

Cloths

Make sure that you get some experience of playing on different tables, so that you can adapt your game when playing on various types of cloth. It will help if you understand some of the differences that you might encounter.

The heavier the cloth the more a spinning ball will drift as a result of the nap. Worn or shaved cloths are easier for the beginner because the cue ball will not drift anywhere near as much when side is imparted. However, because of this, certain billiard shots which actually take advantage of the nap effect, such as jennies, are much more difficult to play. Top players generally find that worn cloths are more of a challenge, especially for shots that make use of the nap.

Shaved cloths are so called because when the cloth is made, the fibres are shaved short, reducing the amount of nap. These cloths are incredibly responsive to stun and screw and many shots will react very differently on these cloths compared to those you may find in the average club. On these superfine cloths the cue ball barely drifts at all when side is imparted; it will push off line (squirt) as it is struck and will often not come back to the same path that it would do on a cloth with a more pronounced nap.

Also, new cloths can be particularly challenging to play on and have some properties that are worthy of note. Firstly, you will find that the pocket jaws of newly covered cushions are receptive to receiving a ball and shots along the cushion are significantly easier on newly covered tables. It is important to note that even though a new cloth will be *more* responsive than a worn one, the cushions will be *less* responsive. Conversely, a worn cloth will be *less* responsive to side and screw while the cushions will be *more* responsive. Also, with new cloths, as a ball rebounds off a cushion it will slip on the bed of the table before starting to roll naturally. This slows a ball down, especially if it hits a cushion square-on.

Cushion slip is a term normally used to describe a ball taking a path closer to the cushion than expected. It is particularly noticeable with new cloths. You can see this effect for yourself if you place the cue ball at the centre of the baulk cushion and aim for a point about 4 inches (10 cm) before the near jaw of the middle pocket. Depending on the amount of slip, the cue ball should hit near to the middle of the top cushion, for strokes played at dead strength.

If a cloth is damp or dirty it will be less responsive to side and screw. Dampness or dirt causes increased friction between the balls and the cloth, which means that any screw or sidespin does not last as long. Conversely, the reason why polishing a cue ball makes it more responsive is because this reduces the friction between the ball and the cloth, so any spin remains for longer. In exhibitions, you might see a player use silicon polish to exaggerate the side or screw effects but don't polish balls and then play a match yourself because the balls will react very strangely indeed.

Cushion response

It is difficult to predict the response from cushions with worn cloths and this can have a significant impact on how you play your game. They often cause a ball to rebound at a faster speed than expected, known as *spring*. If the faces of the cushions are worn, on rebounding, the balls can even *bounce* slightly off the bed of the table. Also, low cushions, chalk on the cue ball or cushion face and uneven cushion rubber are all things that can make cushions unpredictable. Low cushions cause balls to bounce and chalk causes balls to spring.

Realistically, you will not play on good quality match tables all of the time, so you should learn to adjust to less than ideal conditions. If you know that a cushion is unreliable, then allow for it. Obviously, this can be quite frustrating as, if the cushion doesn't spring but you allow for it, your shot will end up short. However, taking an example of a middle-pocket loser, it is much better to leave a long loser afterwards than to leave the object ball in baulk.

Another cause of a faster than usual rebound occurs when an object ball, which is very close to a cushion, is knocked squarely onto it. This effect occurs on all tables and is purely down to ball mechanics. After impact, an object ball will initially skid and if it then hits the cushion while still skidding it will rebound more quickly than normal. Practically speaking, when the cue ball is near an object ball which is close to a cushion you can control the positional aspect by playing at a slow pace. However, at longer distances you might choose to play at a much faster pace to avoid losing position due to a fast rebound. For example, on unfamiliar tables you might choose to bring the object ball in and out of baulk, rather than play a slower shot that could possibly leave it in baulk.

> **In case you were wondering…**
>
> When a skidding ball with no rotation impacts a cushion there will be no ball-cushion friction in the vertical plane to slow the ball down.

It doesn't pay to be too concerned with the type of cushions you are playing on, but it is worth understanding the difference between *steel-backed* cushions and those made out of wood. Steel-backed cushions are commonly believed to be the best type of cushion and are used for most major championships. These cushions have extremely heavy plates of steel bolted to the slate bed of the table, and a wooden section, the wooden cushion part that you see, bolted on to the back of the steel. The rubber is attached to the front face of the steel plate and then covered by the cloth, so of course you don't ever see the steel. The reason that these cushions are preferred is that the extra weight gives a more consistent rebound off the rubber, in general that is. However, a properly fitted wooden cushion, made without any steel plates, will play just as well, assuming that the wood is of a decent density and quality.

If you do play on a poor quality table with light cushions you will find that you have more difficulty controlling the strength of certain shots. For example, a sequence of middle-pocket losers is much more challenging to make if the cushions are poor.

Pocket shape and size

You should adjust your patterns of play depending on the pocket shape and size. If the pockets are exceptionally tight you will need to be more careful and perhaps ignore some standard billiard shots and change your shot selection. It is worth remembering that the pocket shape and size have little consequence on the making of a *cannon*, although on tight tables you may wish to alter the way you play the cannon slightly, so as to avoid leaving balls near cushions. Some pockets are shaped in such a way that makes it exceedingly difficult to get a spinning cue ball *inside* the jaws.

On some tables you might find that certain shots are simply not practical at all. A good example of this is the long jenny, which relies on the pocket accepting a spinning ball. If you feel that your normal shot selection is not the *percentage shot* on a particular table, play something else. It may be that the odds are against you. For example, let's say you could make a long jenny 9 times out of 10 on a table with generous pockets but only 2 times out of 10 on a table with a shaved match cloth and tight pockets; in this case it would be better to change your shot selection.

Balls

One of the most frustrating challenges when playing on different tables is dealing with a poor set of balls. Balls should be well-matched regarding weight, but occasionally you might find that you end up playing with an odd set. Sets of scales that are accurate enough to see if the balls are of equal weight are readily available; there should be no more that 0.5g difference between the lightest and the heaviest ball.

Unfortunately, you will occasionally find a set with a greater variance than this and on these occasions, if you don't have a set of scales and want to check the balls out, perhaps before a match, try playing a long loser from hand with the object ball on the middle spot. Then swap the object ball and cue ball around to see if there is any noticeable difference in the half-ball deflection angle. If you do this with all three balls you should be able to see if there is any inconsistency with their weights—if there is, ask to play with a different set!

You will also come across sets of balls that, despite being evenly matched, throw slightly differently from the angle that you are familiar with. This is quite a common occurrence and it shouldn't take you too long to find the natural angle for each set of balls. Try to determine whether the balls are throwing *narrow* or *wide*, and adjust your setting angle accordingly. You can prepare for this by practising with different sets of balls, rather than playing with the same set all of the time. Nevertheless, under match conditions you might still find it difficult to convince yourself that the natural angle is different from that on your practice table. If the balls are throwing wide, address *very high* to make sure that you are not imparting any unintentional skid on the cue ball. Thereafter, if you miss a long loser because you hit the side cushion pocket jaw, make a mental note of how much wider the balls

> **In case you were wondering...**
>
> The natural angle often varies by a small amount depending on both the table conditions and the set of balls used, and is sometimes referred to as the *split* (of the balls).

are throwing and be sure to adjust the setting angle for the next long loser. It is better to miss the next one by overcompensating and hitting the top cushion jaw, rather than missing on the wide side again. Once you have grasped exactly how the balls are reacting make sure that you adjust the setting angle from hand along with compensating for other half-ball shots. For example, when potting a red to leave a cross-loser, if the balls are throwing wide you will have to make a conscious effort to position the cue ball slightly wider than usual.

Kicks

Perhaps the most exasperating aspect of the game is when you suffer a kick, causing the object ball to travel in a straighter path than intended. You can normally hear the poor contact and the resulting kick will often cause a missed shot. As an example, if you were aiming correctly for a half-ball pot and got a bad kick, you would miss the pot due to not cutting the object ball enough. In addition, the cue ball would throw wider than normal and with a severe kick can visibly be seen to leave the table.

It is worth looking at two types of kick and how you can minimise them. The *chalk kick* is relatively rare but is the worst kick that occurs, happening when a significant amount of chalk coincides with the point of contact between the two balls. With these kicks you will hear a distinct noise at the moment of contact. You can minimize these kicks by limiting the chalking of your cue. The *mini kick* is a more frequent but smaller kick, where the ball often doesn't, but may, jump. It is caused either by a small amount of dirt or chalk at the impact point or surprisingly, by having extremely clean balls. Very clean balls have much higher friction at the point of contact and this is the reason why the balls can sometimes jump when colliding. You can minimize

> **In case you were wondering…**
>
> You might have noticed that, during professional snooker matches, players often have the balls cleaned and then get a kick *immediately* afterwards. Often this is because the balls are extremely clean, causing a significant amount of friction at the point of contact.

these kicks by rotating the cue ball slightly in your hand from time to time, before playing from the **D**, as this will be enough to lubricate the balls slightly and make for a smoother contact between them. This also helps to reduce the occurrence of the relatively rare chalk kicks. It also reduces the build-up of static charge, making the balls less likely to pick up chalk and grit from the table.

Match play

"How is it that top players always seem to play well in matches and yet I never feel that I perform well?" Have you ever asked yourself a similar question? If so, make an effort to do something about it.

The best way to control your emotions is to be self-assured and confident that you have prepared as well as possible. If you have prepared to win, you are likely to win! Even top players perform badly under pressure if they haven't practised for the match. For example, perhaps you find that you are missing a large percentage of long jennies, but haven't had time to practise them. Then, during a match with the scores level and only 10 needed for game, you make a positional slip-up, leaving yourself a long jenny. Under these circumstances you would be unlikely to make the shot, but had you mastered it in practice you would come to the table confident in your ability to win the game.

Always arrive early at the match venue. If you have a long journey, give yourself plenty of time to settle down before your match begins. Try to allow at least 30 minutes to relax before your game. Make sure that you have had some refreshments before you play and if you happen to be playing a tournament with several matches during the day, set aside some time between each match to relax and at least have a light snack.

Make sure that you are ready well before the match is due to start, at least 10 minutes ahead of schedule. You should have a drink available, have your cue ready along with any other equipment you need (such as cue extensions, cloths and chalk) and your coat, keys and any other personal items all appropriately placed with your mobile phone switched off. Find a seat in a suitable location and, while sitting, you should relax and get in the mood for the match.

Avoid negative thoughts and try to think of the positive aspects in all situations. For example, don't get upset if you feel that you have had a bad run of the balls. If your opponent makes one or more flukes it is usually because of poor play and you will eventually get your chances to win. Be positive with your body language and your thoughts; a calm body and a concentrated mind will help you to perform well. For example, if you were 60 behind with 10 minutes to go in a timed match, think positively and look to make up the deficit. Now would be an opportune time to make an 80 break, or perhaps a couple of 40 breaks. Do not think about losing. At the same time, make sure that you conduct yourself well and have a confident and calm manner. Remind yourself that you have prepared well, and that now is the perfect time to put all of your practice into proper use. A good example of when to control your thoughts and body language is after you have missed a seemingly easy opportunity. In these cases, walk calmly back to your seat, relax and think positively. Conversely, if you see your opponent shaking their head in disbelief at a missed shot, or perhaps because of a perceived woeful run of the balls, you can be sure that they are not in the right mood to compete to the best of their ability.

During a match don't fall into the trap of thinking that you aren't playing as well as you should be. It is very common for players to believe that they are at a much better standard than they actually are, leading to a feeling of not performing well. For example, if you can play a sequence of four or five consecutive middle-pocket losers on your own practice table, you should not expect to be able to do the same on an unfamiliar match table. So, if you leave your first in-off short, don't be too critical with yourself. Of course you should endeavour to adapt to the conditions, but in the meantime don't allow yourself to think negatively.

Perhaps the best way to control your emotions is to simply *enjoy playing billiards*. Imagine that you are enjoying a game on your practice table and this should take away much of the pressure of the match. Allow yourself to become totally focussed on the shots that you are faced with and to become utterly engrossed in your patterns of play.

Remember also, that billiards is only a game. Of course, you should have a healthy competitive spirit, a strong desire to win, but losing is not the end of the world. Enjoy the moment of playing this fantastic game!

Index